Utopian Visions

Utopian Visions

By the Editors of Time-Life Books

TIME-LIFE BOOKS, ALEXANDRIA, VIRGINIA

CONTENTS

The Garden of Paradise

Whether as a heavenly realm or an earthly Eden, a state of primeval innocence or perpetual bliss, the concept of paradise is one of the oldest utopian visions. Each culture has depicted paradise its own way, but nearly all share an image of paradise as a garden of eternal spring, wherein the mortal becomes immortal and the human spirit dwells in harmony with the divine.

The word *paradise* is from the Old Persian *pairidaeza,* meaning "park" or "enclosure." It was on the arid Persian plateau that gardens most clearly acquired religious significance. The Persian garden was a walled oasis divided by channels of water—a cosmological idea echoed in the biblical Eden. Symmetrically patterned by fruit trees, flowers, and verdant shrubbery, it was designed as much for philosophical contemplation as physical enjoyment.

The garden paradises of other cultures also embodied eternity. The Koran says that the blessed will be brought to the Lord in "gardens of delight." And the eternal abode of the Hindu gods is a land of flowers, perfumes, and paths of gold.

From celestial roots, the Islamic Prophet's Tree of Bliss grows downward, joining heaven and earth. This eighteenth-century Turkish motif is a version of the mythic Cosmic Tree, a symbol of renewal or immortality.

Judeo-Christian theology likewise invests the garden with paradisiacal qualities. The monastic garden of medieval Europe resembled the Persian garden in being an enclosed retreat. The outside world was impoverished and pestilential; thus the cloister garden with its food crops and medicinal herbs offered some of the fruits of an earthly paradise. In the religious art of that time, the Virgin Mother and Child and other great motifs of Christian belief are often portrayed in walled garden settings.

In the gardens of paradise, Western religions find exaltation; from them, Eastern religions hope for enlightenment. Nature, in Confucian thought, personifies wisdom and virtue. In Zen philosophy, Buddha's presence is assumed in the simplest stone, and according to followers of the Amida Buddhist sect, the path to paradise, the Pure Land, lies through the garden. But by whatever route humankind reaches paradise, and whatever the form paradise takes, the belief endures, as seen in the paintings of paradisiacal gardens on the following pages.

At Allah's behest, angels pay homage to the flame-haloed Adam and Eve in this Koranic view of Eden, from a sixteenth-century Persian miniature (opposite).

In the eighteenth-century Indian painting below, a gopi, or shepherdess, and her companion await the arrival of Krishna, the god of love. A symbol of the human soul seeking union with the Divine—and thus paradise, with its freedom from reincarnation—each gopi believed she alone was the god's beloved. The waiting women are enraptured by the beauty of spring, which signals a time of renewal, awakening human hopes for spiritual consummation and for release from the earthly cycle of birth and rebirth.

In the Indian painting opposite, a richly attired Krishna arrives at full moon to perform his Cosmic Dance. While ethereal helpers rain flowers from above, the gopis form a circle symbolizing the marriage of heaven and earth. The Blue God, as Krishna is also known, dances simultaneously with each gopi; the joining of the couple represents the devotee's embrace of the Divine.

In this 1646 painting titled *Peach Blossom Spring (left), a verdant wild stretches before a lone wayfarer at the picture's right-hand edge. The scene evokes the utopia described by fifth-century Chinese poet T'ao Ch'ien, in which a fisherman comes upon a grove of flowering peach trees. At the end of the grove he passes through a grotto that leads to an enchanted land. He departs this paradise, hoping to return, but he is unable to find his way back.*

The tale reveals the essential Chinese belief that spiritual renewal comes with solitary retreat to nature. In harmony with nature's rhythms and paradoxes, humans can sense within themselves the way to wisdom, truth, and understanding—paradise on earth.

Seeking such harmony, a Japanese official enjoys a meditative moment beneath plum and cherry blossoms in the fourteenth-century scroll above. Rooted in China and transplanted by Buddhist monks, the Japanese garden is a distillation of nature, a place for abstract contemplation, through which the spiritual paradise of Buddhist belief can be glimpsed.

Envisioning paradise as a harmonious land where nature is bountiful, the Florentine artist Sandro Botticelli portrayed the coming of spring in his *Primavera* (below), completed around 1478. The painting depicts Zephyrus, the West Wind (far right in the picture), seizing the veiled Primavera, or Spring, and transforming her into Flora, the petal-scattering goddess of flowers. A melding of classical mythology and Christian symbolism, the artist's eclectic vision reflects the Early Renaissance philosophy that a continuous spiritual circuit joined all creation with God.

At right, a menagerie of creatures, including man and woman, share a bounteous Garden of Eden in this work by Flemish artist Jan Brueghel the Elder. Rendered small and unobtrusive, Adam and Eve recall humankind's original carefree and innocent state and reaffirm the biblical ideal of the fruitful earthly park planted by God.

The peaks and valleys of paradise meld with a sublime sweep into the white light of eternity in British artist John Martin's 1853 painting titled The Plains of Heaven. The landscape illustrates the Christian vision of paradise as it is described in the New Testament's book of Revelation: a lush and ethereal other world, spirited with angels, where souls await the Last Judgment.

CHAPTER 1

In Quest of the Ideal Life

"I**n** Utopia, where every man has a right to everything, they all know that if care is taken to keep the public stores full, no private man can want anything; for among them there is no unequal distribution, so that no man is poor, none in necessity; and though no man has anything, yet they are all rich; for what can make a man so rich as to lead a serene and cheerful life, free from anxieties?"

So did Thomas More, the sixteenth-century English statesman, describe his version of the ideal society and coin the term that would forever be associated with a perfect place. More, who would later become lord chancellor of England during the rule of Henry VIII and a martyr for the Catholic church, wrote *Utopia* in two parts during 1515 and 1516. The title is a play on the Greek word *utopia,* which has the double meaning "good place" and "no place."

It is written in the form of a report by a fictitious Portuguese sailor, Raphael Hythlodaye—another Greek pun, meaning "dispenser of nonsense"—who is described as having made three voyages to the New World with Italian explorer Amerigo Vespucci. The first half of the book consists of a veiled critique of Renaissance England, while the second describes Hythlodaye's visit to the land known as Utopia, an island off the coast of Somewhere, whose "way of life provides not only the happiest basis for a civilized community, but also one which, in all human probability, will last forever."

Thomas More was just one of a long line of visionaries who dreamed of an ideal world, a heaven on earth free from evil and imperfections. Throughout history, brave—and sometimes foolhardy—optimists in nearly every civilization, from ancient Sumerian ruler-priests to Renaissance philosophers to twentieth-century social revisionists, have offered their own versions of this universal dream. Some envisioned a paradise like the Garden of Eden, where humans could live in eternal splendor, free from earthly travails. Others preferred to design their own societies, setting out on paper utopian cities or nations that boasted the perfect solutions to humankind's problems. More's *Utopia* and Plato's *Republic* are among the best-known examples of these blueprints of perfection.

Many have not been content merely to dream or plan their utopias. Rather, they have boldly rejected established society and banded together in their own would-be utopian communities. Members of a sect led by Pythagoras, the sixth-century-BC Greek mathematician and mystic, lived rigidly ascetic lives within monastery-like communities in an attempt to achieve perfection. Later utopians with a spiritual bent would look to the past, to early mystical sects, and to their own magical ideas to guide them in establishing their own paradises on earth.

Two thousand years after Pythagoras's time, countless groups saw the discovery of America as a new beginning, an opportunity to return to an Eden-like existence. Religious utopians established model societies in America that promised the chance to attain spiritual perfection. Others sought to forge in the New World utopian communities ordered on radical intellectual notions. The twentieth century, too, has produced its share of utopian visionaries—including those who believe they live in a New Age and who hold that utopia exists within oneself. By developing the spiritual dimension of human consciousness, they contend, people can live together harmoniously and create a global utopia.

The urge to carve out a bit of heaven on earth has usually been strongest in times of strife and upheaval. For Plato, the catalyst was the fall of his beloved Athens to mighty Sparta; for More, it was signs of the coming Reformation; for many who decided to immigrate to America, it was religious persecution in their homelands; for some twentieth-century Americans, it has been war, poverty, and racial injustice. The quest for utopia shows no sign of abating. Those who study the subject estimate that in the United States alone there are presently no fewer than 3,000 intentional communities—that is, groups that purposely band together in an organized effort to achieve some mutually agreed goals or ideals.

The definition of *utopia* seems to be as varied as the groups that have sought it. For most, however, utopia is perfection, and perfection in this sense is usually defined as harmony—within oneself and with others. But utopias are also concerned with how people should live—addressing such issues as religion, work, equality, sexual mores, family, property, and authority. How the various communities deal with those issues covers a wide range of possibilities. Some see the ideal society as one of material prosperity; others want to be free of material trappings. Utopian visionaries may aspire to a totally natural life, or they may embrace modern technology as fundamental to their communities. Some advocate personal property, but most espouse communal sharing, with equal access to all goods and equal status between all people.

No matter what form it takes, the utopian vision is always with us. As Oscar Wilde wrote, "A map of the world that does not include

Utopia is not worth even glancing at, for it leaves out the one country at which Humanity is always landing. And when Humanity lands there, it looks out, and seeing a better country, sets sail. Progress is the realization of Utopias.''

While the word *utopia* was not used in the context of an ideal society until the Renaissance, the concept of a place free from suffering, where the inhabitants are immortal and forever young, is as old as humankind itself. Every culture has had its paradise myths, as scholars call them, and the paradise myths of the past have piled one on another in the minds of modern humankind, inspiring the secular Western world's vision of utopia.

Many of these myths describe an immemorial golden age where humans lived without fear or want. The Cheyenne Indians, for instance, spoke of a time gone by when men and women cavorted naked and unashamed amid fields of plenty. Other peoples have envisioned paradise as a part of the universe yet unseen, a place that promises a happy existence as a reward after death. In all of these myths, paradise is a place of innocence, free from conflicts. It is also eternal or, if lost for the moment, destined to return in the future.

The Garden of Eden in the Old Testament's book of Genesis, whose images have become part of the consciousness of Western civilization, may be the best-known example of paradise, but it is by no means the earliest recorded description. That distinction belongs to the paradise myth of the Sumerians, the remarkable people who occupied the Tigris-Euphrates valley from about 4000 BC to 2000 BC. Indeed, linguists believe that the Hebrews borrowed the word *eden* (meaning ''fertile plain'') from the Sumerians.

Sumerians were noted for their developments in agriculture, trade, art, architecture, and especially literature. Modern archaeologists have found more than 5,000 tablets and other fragments of objects inscribed with Sumerian literary and religious works.

One tablet has proved particularly fascinating. It told

of the land of Dilmun, a magical place where ''man had no rival.'' The tablet began: The land of Dilmun is pure . . . / It is a clean place, it is a place most bright . . . / In Dilmun the raven utters no cry, / The kite utters not the cry of the kite, / The lion kills not, / The wolf kills not the lamb, / Unknown is the kid-killing dog, / Unknown is the grain-devouring boar . . . / The sick-eyed man says not, ''I am sick-eyed,'' / The old woman says not, ''I am old.''

The legend of Dilmun describes a land that suffers violence from neither wind nor rain, whose fields are eternally green and fruitful, a place where pure waters of the earth spring forth. The idyllic Dilmun is peopled by immortal gods and goddesses who are free from toil and immune to the ravages of age and disease. Yet those who dwell in Dilmun are not immune to temptation. According to the Sumerian legend, the mother goddess Ninhursag caused eight plants to grow among Dilmun's fertile fields, which she forbade the immortals to eat. However, Enki, the god of fresh water, cannot resist sampling the plants. He is stricken with a fatal illness after eating them. Although Nin-

On the fictitious island of Utopia, created by English statesman Thomas More (far left) and depicted in this woodcut from his sixteenth-century book Utopia, life was very different from that of More's Renaissance England. Scholars still debate whether More supported the religious tolerance and communal principles set out in Utopia or whether the book was a satire. The author took great pains to make his story believable—including providing a Utopian alphabet and an example of Utopian verse (below)—yet he filled the text with puns. The name of one city, Amanote, is Greek for "dream town," and the river is called Anider, which means "no water."

hursag saves Enki by creating eight healing goddesses to cure the eight ailing parts of his body, the god's transgression marks the beginning of a new order. From that point on, eternal life is still possible but not inevitable, and a new rank of beings, the "dark-headed" humans, are born to serve as mortal attendants to the gods.

Since the ancestry of the Israelites can be traced to Mesopotamia, it is not surprising to find echoes of Dilmun in the biblical description of the Garden of Eden. Genesis explains that "a river flowed out of Eden to water the garden," which contained "every tree that is pleasant to the sight and good for food." And like the forbidden plants of Dilmun, one tree, heavy with fruit, was forbidden to the garden's inhabitants, Adam and Eve. But Eve was tempted by a serpent, who promised that she and Adam would become like God if they ate an apple from "the tree of the knowledge of good and evil."

"So when the woman saw that the tree was good for food, and that it was a delight to the eyes, and that the tree was to be desired to make one wise, she took of its fruit and ate; and she also gave some to her husband and he ate. Then the eyes of both were opened, and they knew that they were naked; and they sewed fig leaves together and made themselves aprons."

According to Genesis, God punished Adam and Eve for their disobedience, sentencing them to the toil of scratching a living from the land and to eventual death. He then drove them from the garden, exiling them from what had been a state of innocent happiness, of harmony with all God's creatures.

Humankind's fall from grace is not peculiar to Judeo-Christian tradition. There are numerous African myths that relate how human transgressions forced God to return to the heavens. In Angola, for example, the "one great, invisible god, who made all things and controls all things," is known as Nyambi. According to myth, humans "have offended him, and he has withdrawn his affection from them." In North America, Hopi Indian legends tell how the people began to drift away from the Great Spirit, "to divide

According to the Old Testament book of Genesis, the legendary Tower of Babel—envisioned under construction at left by the sixteenth-century Flemish artist Pieter Brueghel the Elder—was built by the descendants of Noah to enable them to reach heaven. Alarmed by such presumptuous behavior, God thwarted the project by confounding the people's language, then scattering them over the face of the earth.

The story offers both an explanation of the origin of the world's many tongues and a warning about the perils of ignoring God's divine plan. Scholars believe the tale's dual messages derive from the similarity between the name Babel—from the Babylonian Babili, or "Gate of God"—and balal, a Hebrew verb meaning "to confuse."

The actual Tower of Babel was probably a ziggurat called E-temen-an-ki, or the "house of the foundations of heaven and earth," which is believed to have been built around the mid-sixteenth century BC in Babylon. Intended as a physical re-creation of the cosmic mountain, which in legend was thought to join the sacred and the profane, the structure rose to a height of about 300 feet. By ascending such ziggurats, Babylonian priests aspired to the symbolic summit of the universe—the point of creation and thus perfection.

and draw away from one another." Then a beguiling serpent invaded their paradise and "led the people still further away from one another and their pristine wisdom. They became suspicious of one another and accused one another wrongfully until they became fierce and warlike and began to fight one another."

In all of these traditions, humankind's fall from grace signaled the end of a golden age, after which the world declined. The belief that the world undergoes a cycle of ages that leads to destruction and regeneration is found in widely different civilizations. In virtually all of these legends, humans are said to have begun life on earth in a state of perfection. One of the best known of these lost ages was the golden age of classical Greek myth, described by the eighth-century-BC Greek poet Hesiod in his epic *Works and Days.* "First of all the immortal gods who have their homes on Olympus created a golden race of mortal men, who lived in the time of Cronus, when he was king in heaven. They lived just like gods, carefree in heart, aloof and apart from toil and sorrow. Wretched old age did not come to them, but, ever strong in legs and arms, they enjoyed themselves with feasts, separated from all evils. They had all good things, for a fruitful earth of its own accord brought forth plentiful and abundant fruit, and they lived happily and peacefully, blessed with many riches. They were wealthy in cattle and were loved by the gods."

According to Hesiod, "when this primeval generation was covered over by the earth" and they had become pure spirits, the gods "created a second race, a race of silver that was inferior by far, resembling the golden race neither in stature nor mind." An even more decadent race of bronze followed—they destroyed themselves by their own hand—and was succeeded by a race of heroes, who died in warfare. The last race—a race of iron—ushered in the current age.

Only one of Hesiod's races—the heroes,

or demigods—gained immortality. Many of them were said to have taken up residence on the Islands of the Blest, also called the Elysian Fields. There they were governed by Cronus and enjoyed freedom from care and sorrow, where "honey-sweet fruit blossoming thrice yearly the grain-giving fields do yield." In Homer's *Odyssey,* the sea god Proteus tells Sparta's King Menelaus he is destined for the Elysian Plain, "where life is easiest for men; there is no snow, for there is neither wintry weather nor ever rain, but always gusts of shrill-blowing Westwind does Ocean send up to refresh men." In Elysium, poets, priests, and heroes pursued their favorite activities free from worries and illness.

Did Hesiod invent this story of the ages of man or was he merely recording an ancient tradition? No one can know for sure. However, the tale of a golden age—and its passing—was accepted as historical fact by most Greeks and Romans. Indeed, generation after generation of Greek and Roman philosophers and poets would reinterpret Hesiod's golden-age mythology.

In Plato's *Laws*—a book written three centuries after Hesiod's time—the author drew on the poet's works. "We must do all we can to imitate the life which is said to have existed in the days of Cronus," Plato wrote, "and in so far as the immortal element dwells in us, to that we must hearken, both in private and public life." The Roman poets Virgil and Ovid, who lived in the first century BC, also based work on Hesiod's legends. In *Metamorphoses,* a collection of narrative poems that long served as a virtual handbook of Greek and Roman mythology, Ovid wrote that in the golden age, "faith and righteousness were cherished by men of their own free will without judges or laws. . . . Without the use of soldiers the peoples in safety enjoyed their sweet repose. . . . Spring was eternal."

The idea that a golden age once existed has always held out to humankind the hope that the paradisiacal era might someday return or be re-created. Like the Greeks, the ancient Indians believed that the world had passed through previous ages, or *yugas*—the Krita, the Treta, and the Dvapara—and that humans were now living in the final, most decadent age, the Kali. They believed the Kali began on February 17, 3102 BC and would end 432,000 years from that date, when a new cycle of ages would commence.

In the Sioux system of belief, the world is protected by a great buffalo "who stands at the gate to the universe and holds back the waters" that periodically threaten the earth. The creature loses a leg with the passing of every age; when all four legs are lost, the legend goes, the world is engulfed and subsequently renewed.

But per-

In this fifteenth-century depiction of his apocalyptic vision, the apostle John glimpses heaven and Satan's marauding forces. From the book of Revelation, the vision previews the final human drama, in which evil is eradicated, and the emergence of a new, harmonious earth. The spiritual center of this realm is the New Jerusalem, which, according to the prophet, descends from heaven to take its place on earth.

A golden beacon of faith, Jerusalem's Dome of the Rock (top), completed in AD 691, shelters the sacred stone (inset) revered by Jews, Christians, and Muslims as a link between paradise and earth. In Judeo-Christian tradition, the rock is where Abraham prepared to sacrifice his son; Muslims believe it is the point from which Muhammad ascended to paradise on his Night Journey. Followers of these religions believe this is where the final judgment will take place.

haps there was no stronger belief in the return of a golden age than that of the Aztec Indians, who banked their empire on it—and lost. According to legend, the Aztec wind god Quetzalcoatl, who dwelled in the city of Tula and ruled over a glorious golden age, was forced by his enemy, the moon god, to leave the city. Quetzalcoatl vowed that he would return one day, however, and would create an even greater paradise for his people. When Spanish explorer Hernán Cortés landed in Mexico in 1519, the Aztecs were convinced that

the Spaniard was the long-expected Quetzalcoatl and that he was returning to govern them. Even the fierce Aztec warrior Montezuma II refused to resist Cortés and his troops.

Many Christians await a return to a golden age, which they believe will manifest itself as a 1,000-year reign of righteousness after Christ's Second Coming. Believers, sometimes called millennialists, cite the New Testament book of Revelation, chapter 20, in which the apostle John describes how for 1,000 years the devil will be restrained and the world will be ruled by Christ and those who have suffered and died for Him. At the end of that time, John relates, the devil will be released, and for a short period will bring misery and chaos to the world.

God will then intervene directly, however, and destroy the devil and his followers; the dead will then rise, and the redeemed will go to live in "a new heaven and a new earth," with a "New Jerusalem." The new earth revealed to John would resemble Eden, with a pure river and a tree of life, whose leaves "were for the healing of the nations." The New Jerusalem—which has become another symbol for hope and rebirth, for escape to paradise—would have "a great high wall" made of jasper (a colored quartz), whose foundations would be "adorned with every jewel." The city itself would be constructed of "pure gold, clear as glass."

Humankind finds itself yearning for and awaiting the return of the golden age because of its own deficiencies. Like Pandora, who could not contain her idle curiosity and released a horde of plagues upon humanity, humans became the despoilers of paradise primarily by failing to maintain spiritual awareness. Thus, Hindus warned that a restless curiosity "lets noble purpose go, and saps the mind, til purpose, mind and man are all undone."

But the possibility of return is always there. As a Manichean writer advised, "Awake, soul of splendor, from the slumber of drunkenness into which thou hast fallen . . . follow me to the place of the exalted earth where thou dwelledst from the beginning." Humans expelled from paradise need not content themselves with dreams of past perfection. They could try to create a new paradise on earth—a utopia, even if only a modest one.

One of the earliest utopian groups was established in Italy during the sixth century BC by the Greek sage Pythagoras. Although he is familiar to many today from the geometric theorem that bears his name, Pythagoras was much more than a great mathematician. He was a philosopher and a mystic and also made important contributions in the fields of music and astronomy. British philosopher Bertrand Russell called Pythagoras "intellectually one of the most important men that ever lived."

Pythagoras was born on the Greek island of Samos in about 580 BC. He was a gifted athlete—winning the heavyweight boxing championship in the 48th Olympic Games—and an eager student. As a youth, he studied with Thales of Miletus, the first of the Hellenic philosophers, and with Anaximander, an admired astronomer and sage.

At Thales's suggestion, Pythagoras, then a young man in his twenties, went to Egypt to learn from that country's fabled temple priests; there he remained for twenty-two years. According to his fourth-century-AD biographer, Iamblichus, Pythagoras spent his time in Egypt "astronomizing and geometrizing, and was initiated, not in a superficial or casual manner, in all the mysteries of the Gods." Iamblichus says Pythagoras also studied for twelve years in Babylon, with the magi. "Through their assistance," Iamblichus relates, Pythagoras "arrived at the summit of arithmetic, music and other disciplines." (Although other sources claim Pythagoras also traveled to India to study with the Brahmans and Britain to study with the Druids, there is no evidence to support these claims.)

Pythagoras returned to Samos at the age of fifty-six. His broad education, with its blend of Eastern spiritualism and Western logic, set him apart from other sages of the time. Others referred to themselves as wise men, Pythagoras was the first to call himself a philosopher, literally a "lover of learning." In fact, for some time the terms *philosopher* and *Pythagorean* were interchangeable.

None of Pythagoras's writings survive, nor is there much written about him by his contemporaries. Indeed, he is mentioned only five times in surviving records from the fifth and fourth centuries BC. As a result, most of what is known about this mysterious, charismatic thinker is owed to later writers, such as Iamblichus, and their impressions are laced with legend.

Stories of his superhuman feats abound. An often-told tale had Pythagoras appearing in two cities at the same

time. "Nearly all historians of his life confidently assert," wrote his biographer, "that in one and the same day he was present at Metapontum in Italy, and Tauromenium in Sicily, and discoursed in common with his disciples in both places." The cities were many days' travel apart.

Pythagoras is also credited with predicting earthquakes, plagues, and violent storms. So attuned was he to nature and the elements that one story says he spoke to a river while crossing it—and that the river replied: "Hail Pythagoras!" Other legends point to the philosopher's mastery over the animal kingdom. A wild bear that had been attacking villagers supposedly became tame when Pythagoras petted it, fed it maize and acorns, and compelled it "by an oath no longer to touch any living thing."

Shortly after returning to Samos, Iamblichus tells us, Pythagoras became disappointed "by the negligence of the Samians in what relates to education." He went to Italy, "conceiving that place to be his proper country, in which men well disposed towards learning were to be found in the greatest abundance." In the southern Italian coastal town of Crotona, Pythagoras established a school that became known as the Pythagorean Society.

The Pythagorean Society was more than a school. It was a utopian brotherhood whose members hoped to usher in a new golden age of wisdom and peace by adhering to the founding philosopher's doctrine and living disciplined, ascetic lives. Initially, about 300 disciples joined the philosopher at Crotona, but soon many more had flocked to the community, lured by Pythagoras's reputation. The society attracted so many followers that it eventually became a formidable political force. It formed a model city ruled by an elite group called the Council of Three Hundred. Offshoots of the community spread outward from Crotona to all the Greek settlements in Italy and most of those in western Greece itself. Everywhere the movement reached, it brought order and cooperation.

The Pythagoreans saw their philosophy as the basis for a way of life that could lead to the salvation of the soul. At the center of their belief were humanity's ties to other life

forms and to the cosmos. This kinship between all of life made possible a conviction that the human soul was immortal. Followers claimed that each soul, or essence, was a fragment of the divine universal soul and that it was imprisoned in a mortal body.

The society's mission was to purify its members' souls for their eventual return to the composite, universal soul. Only by living lives of purity through self-examination, silence, and rigid adherence to the rules could a member prepare for the coming golden age. However, since the study of philosophy alone could not fully explain the world, the study of mathematics was deemed indispensable for all intellectual and spiritual progress.

Aspirants for membership underwent a rigorous initiation. First, they had to pass Pythagoras's scrutiny of everything, from how they treated their parents to "their unseasonable laughter" to "their mode of walking and the whole motion of their body." If an aspirant passed this test, he was purposely neglected by Pythagoras for three years while the philosopher noted how the initiate "was disposed with respect to stability, and a true love of learning."

Once accepted as a candidate, the initiate had to observe a five-year vow of silence and was stripped of all his possessions. If he passed the society's tests—including rigorous mental exercises—he was dubbed an "esoteric" and was permitted to join Pythagoras's inner circle of disciples. If rejected, the initiate was given double the wealth he had brought in with him and, as Iamblichus notes, "a tomb was raised to him as if he were dead."

Initiates were divided into two classes based on their abilities and circumstances. The *mathematici* (also known as the Pythagoreans) formed the brotherhood's inner circle and concerned themselves with matters of logic and cosmology; the *acusmatici* (also called the Pythagorists) studied ethics and religion. The groups met together for instruction. Typical sessions included discussion of such philosophical questions as: What is the most just thing? (Answer: to sacrifice.) Or: What is the wisest thing? (Answer: numbers.) Initiates would also hear words of wisdom:

"Do not assist a man in laying a burden down; for it is not proper to be the cause of not laboring; but assist him in taking it up." Or: "To him who asks for counsel, give no other advice than that which is the best; for counsel is a sacred thing."

Like monks, Pythagoreans followed rigidly structured lives. They wore white, nonwoolen garments and slept on bed coverlets of the same cloth. Each morning before arising, they exercised their memories by recalling all the events of the previous day in order. Then came a walk in silence, since they believed it was not proper to converse until each had calmed his own soul and harmonized with reason. The rest of the day was filled with strict routines of study and labor.

Since they believed in metempsychosis—the transmigration of the soul from one body to another, animal or human—and did not wish to harm the body in which any soul resided, Pythagoreans were strict vegetarians. Even certain vegetables, such as beans, were not eaten or touched in any way, because as spermatic plants they were symbols of generation. Such prohibitions were taken to extremes. Legend has it that a group of Pythagoreans, besieged by an enemy, once fought to the death when they could have easily escaped by crossing a bean field.

Pythagoras placed much emphasis on harmony, explaining that man had to reconcile the conflicting forces hidden within the body. Exploring the purity of music and mathematics were ways of achieving this harmony, as was developing the bonds of friendship. In friendship, taught Pythagoras, one must always remain loyal.

To illustrate this point, Iamblichus tells the story of the Pythagoreans Lysis and Euryphamus. After he had just completed his devotions

In this Tibetan painting from the 1800s, a divine couple make love according to the philosophy of Tantrism, a mystical religion that influenced some Buddhist sects. Tantrism holds that through a ritualized process of yoga, meditation, offerings, and sexual intercourse—which represents ultimate bliss and the creation of a harmonious unit—humans can transcend purely carnal sensations and experience an exalted state of knowledge. The Buddhas surrounding the pair symbolize the center of the cosmos and the four directions.

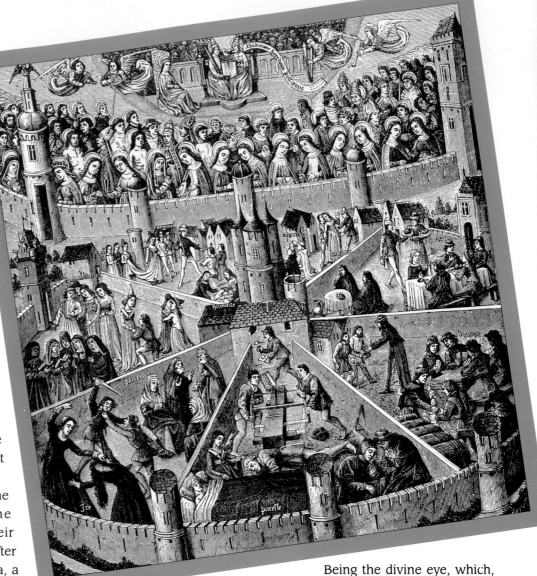

at the temple of Juno, Lysis met his friend Euryphamus, who was about to enter the temple. Euryphamus asked his friend to wait for him. Lysis agreed and took a seat outside the temple. However, after Euryphamus finished his prayers, he forgot about Lysis and left the temple through another gate. "But Lysis waited for him without quitting his seat," wrote Iamblichus, "the remainder of that day and the following night, and also the greater part of the next day."

With such devotion to duty and one another, it seems ironic that the Pythagoreans became victims of their own success. Yet some thirty years after the community was founded at Crotona, a rejected initiate helped turn public opinion against the Pythagorean Society by assailing its exclusive, oligarchical nature. Subsequently, politicians and many of the common folk came to resent the power of the society. Its meeting places were attacked and some of its members—possibly including Pythagoras himself—were murdered. Charges of heresy and subversion were leveled at the Pythagoreans, and their fall from power was swift and tragic. Scattered survivors of the society, however, would maintain their founder's beliefs for the next five centuries.

Although his attempt to create a utopian society that sought the perfection of the spirit and the mind ultimately failed, Pythagoras's accomplishments live on. There is perhaps no more fitting epitaph to his life than that provided by Iamblichus: "He brought about for his disciples converse with the gods. . . . He purified and restored the soul. He revived and evoked its divine part. He directed to the centre of

Being the divine eye, which, as Plato asserts, is more worth saving than ten thousand corporeal eyes . . . for through it, we apprehend the one Truth."

In about 387 BC, more than 100 years after the death of Pythagoras, a young Greek sailed from Athens to southern Italy to meet with some Pythagoreans. Like others before him, he had come in the hope of finding answers to questions that were troubling him. "I had once been full of enthusiasm for public service," he explained. "Now when I concentrated on the political scene and observed its general chaos I ended by feeling dizzy. . . . I came to realize that every single state suffers from bad government." The visitor had reason to be troubled. What in retrospect is viewed as Greece's most glorious era had finally come to an end with the deaths of the venerable philosopher Socrates and the great tragedians Euripides and Sophocles. Once-proud Athens had only recently suffered a crushing defeat by Sparta in the Peloponnesian War, which had lasted almost three decades. The state was politically and economically ravaged. Could the Pythagoreans help the young Plato find calm in the wake of this storm?

The time Plato spent with the Pythagoreans—delving into their philosophy and examining their utopian community—seems to have changed his life. Intellectually revitalized, he returned to Athens within a year and founded the Academy, his school for statesmen, and wrote the first of his philosophical masterpieces, *Phaedo*. During this period, Plato also wrote the work that many people consider to be the finest example of a literary description of a utopian society, *The Republic*.

The Republic is a brilliant defense of Plato's conception of the ideal state. Written at a time when Greek political life was in disarray, *The Republic* was Plato's vehicle to voice his displeasure over state policy as well as a philosophical treatise on justice. But to some scholars, Plato's ideal society is also a metaphor for the ideal or perfect soul, and the path outlined in *The Republic* leads to a goal of spiritual rather than social enlightenment.

The work took the shape of a dialogue between Socrates, Plato's former teacher, and various friends. As they attempted to answer the question, What is justice?, they formulated what they considered to be the ideal society. If they could understand what a state needed in order to be just, the philosophers reasoned, they should be able to generalize and understand justice itself.

"We are forming a happy state," wrote Plato, "not picking out some few persons to make them alone happy, but are establishing the universal happiness of the whole." To guarantee this happiness, he concluded, the ideal state must contain the same virtues that nourish the soul—wisdom, bravery, temperance, and justice. To establish a strong government, it is necessary to choose rulers who are capable of ruling, Plato reasoned. "The truth established by nature is that he who is ill, whether he be rich or poor, ought to wait at the doctor's door, and every man who needs to be ruled, at the door of him who can rule."

In Plato's utopian city-state, modeled in part on Sparta, Athens's nemesis, there were three orders of citizens: Guardians, who ruled and advised the rest; Auxiliaries, who had executive and military responsibilities; and Workers, who included farmers, artisans, and traders. If each class performed its duties as expected, wrote Plato, the state should reach the ideals of justice and happiness.

Despite the contrived caste system, all of the several thousand residents of Plato's utopian city-state would share in the community's wealth. Private wealth is always corrupting, Plato held, and if people plunged into "unbounded acquisition" of it, the city-state was bound to suffer. Therefore, in the Republic, the Guardians and Auxiliaries would own all of the community's property in common. The communal utopia would prosper when "the largest number of men agree in applying these words, 'mine' or 'not mine' to the same thing," wrote Plato.

Plato painted an idyllic portrait of his paradise, where everyone enjoys life's simple pleasures. "I presume that they will produce corn and wine, and clothes and shoes, and build themselves houses. . . . They will live on barley and wheat," he wrote, and "make merry themselves and their children, drinking their wine, wearing garlands, and singing the praises of the gods, enjoying one another's society, and not begetting children beyond their means, through a prudent fear of poverty and war."

To foster unity, Plato outlawed marriage for the Guardians and Auxiliaries and proposed that they possess their wives in common. "No one," Plato determined, "shall have a wife of his own; likewise the children shall be in common and the parent shall not know his child, nor the child the parent." Breeding was to be overseen by the Guardians, and only the best specimens—based on such attributes as age, strength, education, and appearance—were to be chosen for mating. Newborn children were to be taken away from their mothers and housed in a community nursery, freeing the women of Plato's aristocracy from the duties of bringing them up. If the women happened to be of

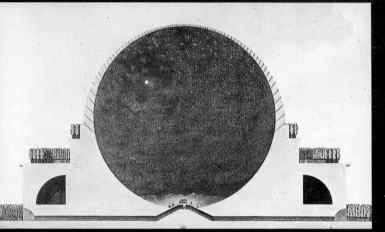

In an eighteenth-century design that
calls to mind twentieth-century architectural
styles, architect Étienne-Louis Boullée
sought to honor the natural philosopher and
scientist Isaac Newton by creating this
futuristic cenotaph in 1784. Boullée's concept, based on the utopian belief that
everything in nature has a particular nature
of its own, relied on simple geometric
forms. An exterior view of the monument
(top) depicts a terraced base cradling
an immense sphere, symbolizing the universe. Envisioned at night, a cross
section of the structure reveals holes in the
sphere's vaulted ceiling, which create
the illusion of stars (above, left). In another
cross section, a glowing lamp within
an armillary sphere, suspended from the
globe's center, creates a daylight
effect (above, right).

the Guardian class, they were expected to help the men rule the city-state.

Plato also laid down strict guidelines for education and took a cue from the Pythagoreans when he stressed the importance of musical training. "Rhythm and harmony sink most deeply into the inner recesses of the soul," wrote Plato, "and take most powerful hold of it, bringing gracefulness in its train, and making a man graceful if he be nurtured, but if not, the reverse." All music, literature, painting, and architecture must meet certain ethical standards, asserted Plato. Art is intended to serve the interests of the state, he held, not express the whims of its creator.

Many see the Republic's lack of personal freedom, rule by elites, and dissolution of the family as the hallmarks of a totalitarian state. Nevertheless, over the centuries since it was written, countless thinkers have been inspired by the philosophical ideals that form the foundation of this lively utopia. In his 1923 landmark study entitled *The History of Utopian Thought,* Joyce Oramel Hertzler wrote that Plato "conceived of philosophy as being an instrument, not merely for the interpretation, but for the remolding of society. The 'Republic' is not vague and fantastic, but full of hope and inspiration."

To its creator, the idealized city-state remained a vision of perfection, an unattainable ideal. Plato did not claim that his utopian plan could be realized on earth but believed it contained ideals and principles that politicians should strive for. He wrote that his utopia "exists in our reasoning, since it is nowhere on earth, at least as I imagine. But in heaven, probably, there is a model of it."

Just as Plato adopted—and adapted—many Pythagorean beliefs as he developed his concept of the perfect city-state in *The Republic* and elsewhere, many others were inspired by the utopian teachings of the mystical seer from Samos. Virgil's *Aeneid,* published after his death in 19 BC, includes a moving description of the Pythagorean concept of the afterlife. And Plutarch, whose first-century-BC work *Life of Lycurgus* contains an idealized depiction of Sparta, was a Pythagorean. Entire communities also drew inspiration from the long-vanished utopian Pythagorean Societies. Indeed, some patterned themselves so closely after the Pythagoreans that they were described as Neo-Pythagoreans. Among these was a mystery cult of ancient Palestinian Jews known as the Essenes.

"These men live the same kind of life as do those whom the Greeks call Pythagoreans," claimed first-century Jewish historian Josephus of one of the many Essene communities that flourished in Palestine and Syria from the second century BC to the second century AD. The comparison was understandable, for the Essenes, like the Pythagoreans, lived in strict monastery-like communities and shared the same utopian goal of perfection.

The Essenes believed that the apocalypse was imminent and foresaw an end to the world similar to that later envisioned by millennialists. They viewed life as an ongoing battle between the opposing forces of the Sons of Light, representing truth and piety, and the Sons of Darkness, who constituted evil. Every being, from man to the angels, is a member of one of these two camps, claimed the Essenes, and the struggle between them will continue until the world ends. Then, on Judgment day, the Sons of Light will emerge victorious. Next, an apocalyptic "war of the mighty ones of the heavens will spread throughout the world," and all creation will be devastated. Evil will be banished and the righteous will enjoy "everlasting joy in the life of eternity, and a crown of glory with raiment of majesty in everlasting light."

To prepare themselves for this cataclysmic spiritual battle, the Essenes rejected society, often establishing themselves in the desert or other desolate regions. There, living strictly ordered lives of self-denial, they prepared their bodies and souls for God's final battle.

Like the Pythagoreans, the Essenes surrendered all their possessions when they joined the community and, as Josephus noted, "the wealthy man receives no more enjoyment from his property than the man who possesses nothing." Most members were celibate, and with few exceptions

A Scientist Who Talked with Angels

Emanuel Swedenborg devoted his life to the pursuit of knowledge. That quest led the respected eighteenth-century Swedish scientist, philosopher, and theologian into many different arenas, but none were as challenging to him as the realm of the spiritual.

In April 1744, Swedenborg began experiencing a series of remarkable dreams and visions, in which he allegedly traveled into the afterlife, walked with God along the paths of paradise, and spoke with angels. In what he described as simple conversations, Swedenborg learned that spirits were much like humans. They live in a world that exists between heaven and earth, residing in communities with people of similar character. But unlike life on earth, where such frailties as greed and hypocrisy are often hidden, all foibles are revealed in the spiritual realm. Under the tutelage of angels, however, spirits try to perfect themselves, in hopes of becoming angels. In essence, Swedenborg discovered, the soul's fate depended not on God's final judgment but on the spirit's bent toward perfection or destruction.

Swedenborg relayed his findings in massive volumes written with a scientist's diligence: "I recount the things I have seen. I write you down a plain statement of journeys and conversations in the spiritual world. I have proceeded by observation and induction as strict as that of any man of science among you."

Although Swedenborg gained few followers in his lifetime, his beliefs in the spirit's perfectibility and in earth's spiritual counterpart eventually established him as an influential force in the search for the utopian ideal. The New Jerusalem church that his disciples founded in 1787, and the many societies based on his teachings, thrive throughout the world today.

women were excluded from the monastic settlements. Aspirants had to pass through four stages or grades before they were admitted into the community. Only when the applicant was judged spiritually fit would he be admitted, a process that usually took five years.

Once admitted, initiates found life within a typical Essene community rigorous and highly structured. The discovery in Israel in 1947 of a six-foot long, first-century-BC parchment scroll referred to as the Manual of Discipline provided insight into the sect's laws, philosophy, and daily rituals. According to the manual—part of what have come to be known as the Dead Sea Scrolls—members rose before dawn and offered prayers to the sun, celebrating the seven great cycles of creation. After prayers they went to their jobs. The monastery was totally self-sufficient, and duties ranged from farming and baking to pottery making and copying out sacred texts.

The members assembled again at midday for a purifying cold bath and a meal, during which silence was observed. They then returned to their jobs until time for the evening meal. The Manual of Discipline outlined proper behavior at such gatherings: "The priest shall be seated first and the elders second, then all the rest of the people. . . . A man shall not speak in the midst of his neighbor's words. . . . And further, he shall not speak before his position which is written before him. The man who is asked shall speak in his turn; and . . . a man shall not speak a word which is not to the liking of the masters."

The Sabbath was strictly observed; members were even forbidden to excrete bodily wastes that day lest they profane the Sabbath. An Essene who failed to correctly observe the holy day was banished from the sect for seven years. Other punishments were dispensed to enforce discipline; these included reducing food rations and denying members participation in the community's sacramental rituals. Falling asleep in the assembly earned thirty days of punishment, fraud sixty days, gossiping one year. Swearing, gossiping about the masters, or staying in touch with an excommunicate earned immediate and irrevocable expulsion. Members apparently feared excommunication more than death. Josephus reported that those who were banished from the community often simply lay down in the desert and died.

The Essenes considered slavery to be unjust and did not own slaves. According to Philo, a first-century Jewish philosopher from Alexandria, "they denounce owners of slaves, not merely for their injustice in outraging the laws of equality, but also for their impiety in nulling the statute of Nature." It is believed that the Essenes often bought slaves from others and then freed them.

Although there is no reference to the Essenes in the New Testament, the sect flourished and by Jesus' time probably numbered around 4,000 followers. (Some scholars believe that John the Baptist may have spent some time with the Essenes at Qumran.) They maintained their distance from other Jews—believing themselves to be the only true Israel—and lived in tightly knit communities. Describing themselves as the elect, the Lord's chosen troops on earth, they kept themselves in constant readiness for their role on Judgment Day. By fashioning what they considered to be an earthly utopia and purifying their soul within it, the Essenes hoped to help usher in a heavenly, everlasting paradise.

The Essenes and the Pythagoreans shared more than similar philosophical ideals, they shared the same destiny. Both movements eventually disappeared, victims of the ravages of time and adversaries who condemned their elitism. Countless other utopian communities have suffered similar fates; many are mere footnotes in the pages of history, others are long for-

Looking Back to a Better World

To nineteenth-century social idealist John Ruskin, England had lost much with the coming of the industrial age. He abhorred everything about the mass-production era, believing only artisans were engaged in noble work. He felt people were demeaned by machines and realized their full potential only through creativity. Tasks begun and finished as a whole enhance the human experience, he said, and contribute to harmonious lives for all.

He yearned for medieval England—an era he saw as congenial and well ordered. Ruskin expressed that view in *The Stones of Venice* in 1853. "We have much studied and much perfected, of late, the great civilized invention of the division of labour; only we give it a false name. It is not, truly speaking, the labour that is divided, but the man . . . broken into small fragments and crumbs of life; so that all the little piece of intelligence that is left in a man is not enough to make a pin, or a nail, but exhausts itself in making the point of a pin or the head of a nail."

In 1871, realizing that industry was not going away, Ruskin founded the Guild of Saint George, a model industry that would buy land and factories and operate them along socialist lines. He also established an arts and science museum at Sheffield.

Although only the museum survived, Ruskin's efforts were not in vain. He inspired many like-minded individuals, including those who organized the arts and crafts movement and the Pre-Raphaelite Brotherhood of painters *(overleaf)*, and he contributed to working-class education. A number of societies were founded to pursue Ruskin's ideals, and a college in his name was established at Oxford University.

Heartbreak in Camelot

Few followers of John Ruskin were as devoted to utopian visions of medieval times as author and artist William Morris *(left)*. Morris, who became known for his wallpaper prints *(background)*, sought to re-create the past. He founded the arts and crafts movement to promote the use of handmade items and developed a program to revive the guild system.

Morris emulated medieval painters in his own work and was fascinated by medieval literature, particularly Thomas Malory's fifteenth-century *Morte d'Arthur*, a group of tales centered on the legendary King Arthur. He shared his devotion to Arthurian times with his friend Dante Gabriel Rossetti *(overleaf)*, a founder of the Pre-Raphaelite school of painting. Morris and Rossetti also shared a love for a working-class girl named Jane Burden who sat for both as an artist's model.

Rossetti and Jane were deeply in love. But he, betrothed to another, persuaded Jane to marry Morris. However, Jane was unhappy with the shy, awkward Morris. It was boisterous, romantic Rossetti she adored. And he adored her, spending much time with her and repeatedly painting her portrait; even his paintings of knights were said to be Jane in costume.

William Morris lived apart from his wife for much of their marriage, quietly acceding to the passion she and Rossetti shared. Morris had cherished a romantic notion of medieval times; he could not foresee how closely his life was to parallel the love triangle of Arthurian legend.

As if previewing the future, Jane Burden appears as Guinevere in this 1858 painting by her soon-to-be-husband, William Morris. Besotted by the dark-eyed beauty, who came to embody the Pre-Raphaelite ideal, Morris is said to have scrawled on the canvas, "I cannot paint you but I love you." Guinevere is Morris's one surviving oil painting.

Artist Dante Gabriel Rossetti (above) offers a stunning tribute to Jane Burden Morris in this 1877 painting titled Astarte Syriaca. Astarte was the Syrian Aphrodite, and Rossetti attempted to portray Jane as a sort of forbidden object of worship, shadowy and somber and even more enticing than the goddess of love and beauty.

gotten. However, there are centuries-old utopias that seem as vibrant today as when they were first created. Their elaborate visions of a perfect world continue to be debated by intellectuals and eager experimenters. These are, of course, the utopias that existed only in the minds of their creators and survive today on the pages of well-thumbed books. Like Plato's *Republic,* the best-known ancient example of utopian literature, and Sir Thomas More's *Utopia,* such blueprints for perfection found eager audiences over the centuries. According to turn-of-the-century French novelist Anatole France, "without the Utopias of other times, men would still live in caves, miserable and naked. It was Utopians who traced the lines of the first city. . . . Out of generous dreams come beneficial realities. Utopia is the principle of all progress, and the essay into a better future."

One such essay is Saint Augustine's *City of God,* written between AD 413 and 426 as a response to those who blamed the fall of the Roman Empire on the weakening influence of Christianity. To silence the Church's critics, Augustine distinguished in his work between two realms—the City of Man and the City of God—thus creating the concept of separation between church and state. The City of God, wrote Augustine, was a utopia where order and virtue prevailed, whereas the City of Man was chaotic and replete with the frailties of human nature. Instead of blaming the Church for the state's earthly failings, Augustine reasoned, humans should look on it as a safe haven, an earthly representative of the utopian City of God.

Although the *City of God* was drawn mostly from the Judeo-Christian tradition and contained little original thinking, it was a very influential work. Indeed, its conception of the separation between church and state paved the way for the Church's domination of Europe. As Joyce Hertzler notes in *History of Utopian Thought,* the *City of God* "played an important part in the plans of kings and popes, and the schemes of empires and hierarchies."

Nearly eleven centuries passed between Saint Augustine's *City of God* and the next great utopian work, Thomas More's *Utopia*. Thomas More lived in remarkable times. He was born in 1478 during the flowering of the Renaissance and lived through the Reformation. Erasmus, Martin Luther, Machiavelli, the Medicis, Michelangelo, Leonardo da Vinci, and Raphael were his contemporaries. Scholars had recently introduced classics of the ancient world to the West and opened broad new avenues of learning to their eager students. The invention of printing promised to be even more enlightening. There seemed to be no limits to this rebirth of learning. Even the world itself—or at least humankind's conception of it—was in flux as the explorers Vasco da Gama, Christopher Columbus, John Cabot, and Amerigo Vespucci discovered new lands and redrew the medieval maps. It was in such a heady atmosphere that Thomas More conceived his perfect community.

Thomas More studied the classics, including Plato and Saint Augustine, and he trained as a lawyer. A brilliant student, he came to be regarded as one of the foremost scholars of his time. Although he later served as lord chancellor of England and gave up his life in defense of the Church, he is mostly remembered for *Utopia*.

In More's Utopia, a crescent-shaped island off the coast of Somewhere, the government is a democracy, headed by a prince elected for life. Education is greatly emphasized. There are so few laws that lawyers are unnecessary. The family is strong and sacrosanct. Adults are monogamous, and divorce is allowed only in extreme circumstances. Those who engage in premarital sex forfeit the right to marry at all, and adulterers are sentenced to slavery. Each urban household consists of at least ten adults and their children; in the country, there are at least forty adults in each home. Houses are identical and each one has a garden. Doors have no locks. Everyone works just six hours a day in Utopia, three hours before lunch and three after. All are engaged in trades, and all goods produced are stored in a communal warehouse. From there, residents collect whatever they need.

Since money is not needed in Utopia, owning gold and silver is forbidden. To demonstrate the foolishness of

Led by little children, predators and prey huddle quietly together in Edward Hicks's nineteenth-century painting The Peaceable Kingdom. One of more than 100 works the artist based on a biblical passage extolling universal brotherhood, the painting symbolizes the idea of America as a paradise where all creatures live in harmony: In the background, William Penn and the Indians sign the 1681 treaty that led to the founding of Pennsylvania, which Penn envisioned as a utopian haven for the Quakers.

hoarding precious metals, Utopians use them for common household utensils or even as chains for slaves. Utopians wondered how people in other countries could place so high a value on something as worthless as gold. How, they asked, could "a lumpish, block-headed churl, who hath no more wit than an ass . . . have nevertheless many wise and good men in subjection and bondage, only . . . because he hath a great heap of gold."

Utopians detest war. "They, in opposition to the sentiments of almost all other nations, think that there is nothing more inglorious than that glory that is gained by war," More wrote. While Utopians would fight in defense of their country, they would prefer to hire others to fight for them. Even hunting was considered barbarous.

More's *Utopia* was an intellectual exploration of an ideal society. In contrast, *City of the Sun,* the work of Italian philosopher, monk, poet, and astrologer Tommaso Campanella, was part of a practical campaign to unite the world under the authority of Spanish rule. Written in 1602, less than a century after the appearance of *Utopia, City of the Sun* summed up Campanella's ideas for a new world order, one that would lead to a higher standard of living for all people, a unification of the peoples of the world under the Spanish, and a reformation of the Church. Campanella's radical ideas had first become known years before he decided to commit them to paper, and he was consequently arrested as a heretic, imprisoned, and tortured during the Spanish Inquisition. Campanella wrote *City of the Sun* while serving a life sentence in prison.

Austrinopolis, the city of the book's title, reflects the author's interest in astrology and science. "It is divided into seven large rings or circles named after the seven planets," he wrote, with each ring "connected to the next by four streets passing through four gates facing the four points of the compass." Within each circle were painted illustrations representing the sciences, so that the city itself was like an open textbook. At the center of the city stood a temple from which astrologers read the skies. "It is their duty to observe the stars and their movements," explained Campanella,

"and to know all about their effects on human affairs and their powers."

Campanella's ideal state, like More's and Plato's, was based on communal sharing. Its citizens were "rich because they want nothing, poor because they possess nothing." Strict codes dictated who could marry and bear children, how work was to be divided, and how the utopia's residents were to be educated. Unlike other utopian visions, Austrinopolis was an autocratic monarchy ruled by a chief priest and his assistants, who controlled all major facets of the community. And in contrast to Thomas More's utopia, whose foundations were based on morality as well as a strong family unit, Campanella believed in science and absolute rule. Family love and loyalty were replaced by love for the state.

Increasingly, science became an important factor in literary utopias. *Christianopolis,* a utopian work by German social reformer and Lutheran minister Johann Valentin Andreae, was published in 1619. Written in the form of a letter, *Christianopolis* was designed around the concept "To be wise and to work are not incompatible, if there is moderation." On first glance, Christianopolis seems just another Renaissance utopian city-state, but Andreae added a new wrinkle; he closely linked work and science. Although the community's first aim, as its name implies, was worship, learning was highly emphasized. "Unless you analyze matter by experiment, unless you improve the deficiencies of knowledge by more capable instruments you are worthless," wrote Andreae. In his model city, science was the "testing of nature herself."

Science, more so than religion, was the focal point of *New Atlantis,* an unfinished utopian treatise published in 1627 by Andreae's English contemporary, Francis Bacon. Bacon's work described an imaginary South Seas island ruled by a wise king who had organized the utopia on the basis of applied science. Fittingly, the island's most important institution was Solomon's House, or the College of Six Days' Work, a scientific foundation that was virtually a state within a state, "the lantern of this kingdom."

Bacon himself was a natural scientist, and this background becomes apparent when he describes the scientific riches found in the utopia's college. There are countless laboratories, medicine shops, astronomical observatories, zoological gardens, "mechanical arts which you have not, and stuffs made by them, as papers, linen, silks, tissues, dainty works of feathers of wonderful lustre, excellent dyes." Bacon also explained that the islanders have already mastered the art of flying and building submarines—not to mention the fact that they have discovered the secret of perpetual motion.

In spite of his enthusiasm, however, Bacon's *New Atlantis* tends to disappoint as utopian literature. In the end, it is little more than an essay on the necessity of organization and planning; the political and social needs of humans are quickly dispensed with, and their spiritual needs are not addressed. Bacon had his reasons for focusing on science in his work, however; he believed that if people could be taught to examine almost any problem from an impersonal, scientific point of view, there would be harmony and happiness in the society.

Since the first telling of the Dilmun paradise myth, since Plato took pen to papyrus and produced *The Republic,* the urge to reach deep into one's own imagination and fashion a perfect society has proved irresistible to hundreds of thinkers. This growing collection of utopian legends and literature has long offered enthusiasts the chance to momentarily lose themselves in the tantalizing world of "what if?" and imagine living on the Greeks' Islands of the Blest or in More's Utopia. But for many, the desire to reject the established order and chase the elusive dream of perfection could be realized only by actually putting the utopian theories of these works into practice. Under the guidance of charismatic and sometimes mystic visionaries, utopian communities were formed. To scores of these hopeful pioneers, one land above all others beckoned. Some called it simply the New Land, some the promised land, others called it by name—America.

Builders of Backyard Utopias

I could see these designs in my mind, and these beautiful symbols. I knew they represented the universe and its forces and the great powers that hold all of this planet here together." Thus did self-taught artist Eddie Owens Martin describe the inspiration that impelled him to create his own architectural utopia. Driven by his inner visions, he worked for years to transform four acres of rural Georgia into a rambling complex of cement temples and fortress walls vividly aglow with mystical motifs, including the pyramids, moon, and stars seen above.

In giving concrete reality to the structures that shimmered in his mind's eye, Martin joined a scattered band of naive visionaries, individuals with little or no artistic training who answer an irrepressible inner need to fashion their small corners of the world into personal versions of paradise. They say they are responding to waking visions or dreams, to the specific dictates of spirits, or simply to their own mystical philosophy of life.

As seen on these pages, some of their creations suggest ancient shrines; others are phantasmagorical concoctions of cast-off junk. These utopia builders frequently face derision from neighbors who do not share their visions—although once in a while they receive kind of public vindication in the form of approval from the artistic establishment. Neither scorn nor praise seems to make any difference to most of them. They continue to embellish their fanciful environments as refuges against the outside world and as physical embodiments of their intensely personal ideals.

A Postman's Palace of Dreams

To amuse himself while making his daily rounds in the province of Drôme, French postman Ferdinand Cheval daydreamed about building a wondrous palace that would embody "all the former architectures of primitive times" and thus "outstrip the imagination." Cheval's castle in the air remained just that for some ten years. Then one day in 1879, he came across such a beautiful stone that he was inspired to turn his fantasy into reality.

From that moment on, Cheval was a man possessed. He would spy unusual bits of rock while on his postal rounds and later collect them in a wheelbarrow and haul them back to his garden. There he incorporated the stones into a mélange of towers, stairways, temples, grottoes, waterfalls, and sculptures. Growing ever more enchanted with his creation, Cheval—who had never before touched trowel or chisel—decided the structure would be his tomb, a monument that would grant him a measure of immortality.

After more than thirty years of single-handed labor, the so-called Ideal Palace stood complete—thirty-five feet tall and eighty-five feet long, a utopian dream realized in stone and cement *(below).* Although his neighbors ridiculed Cheval's palace and he was prohibited by law from being buried in it, Cheval gloried in his paradise until his death in 1924. His handiwork is now a national monument.

Ferdinand Cheval (left and with his wife below) called on his imagination and memories of places fictional and real to create the Ideal Palace. The structure, which includes Hindu-style temples and a mosque, is embellished with reliefs, mosaics, and sculptures depicting exotic plants and animals, biblical scenes, and Egyptian-style mummies (inset, below).

St. EOM is pictured here in one of his self-made costumes. He said that a spirit guided his hand in the building of Pasa-quan, and he referred to the figures guarding its entrance (below) as the people of Mu—a refer-ence to the legendary sunken continent some scholars have linked with the Garden of Eden.

When Eddie Owens Martin was living in New York in 1935, the fortuneteller claimed a voice from the spirit world informed him that he was to be the start of something new. "You'll call yourself St. EOM," the voice instructed, pronouncing Martin's acronym as ohm, "and you'll be a Pasaquoyan— the first one in the world."

But not until years later did the Georgia-born Martin figure out what a Pasaquoyan was—one who brings the past and the future together—and it was 1957 before he began to fulfill his mysterious calling. That year he moved back to Georgia and began transforming the house and land his mother had left him in Buena Vista into the fortress he named Pasaquan.

St. EOM, as Martin thenceforth called himself, said he built Pasaquan as "a monument to all the primitive peoples in the world." Indeed, its style reflects his intentions: The colorful designs look Indian, African, or Oriental. But more than anything, the densely decorated walls and buildings *(below and lower inset)* served as a refuge for its eccentric creator. "After I got these walls put up, then I felt I had the world shut out," Martin remarked before his death in 1986. "Here I can be in my own world . . . and wherever I look, I see something beautiful."

The Reverend Howard Finster (right) claims that "this could be an eternal planet if all the people actually come to God." He views his art—which includes Paradise Garden (below) and the World's Folk Art Church (lower inset)—as a means to spread this message.

48

Sacred Art in a Homemade Paradise

"God sent me here to be a man of visions," evangelical preacher and self-taught artist Howard Finster once remarked, "and to tell the world about my visions through my sacred art and my garden." In the early 1960s, Finster began transforming the two acres behind his house in Pennville, Georgia, into a surreal scene of makeshift monuments, bottle houses, and cement hills encrusted with mirrors and religious sculptures. A hand-lettered sign in what is now popularly called Paradise Garden explains its creator's goal: "I built this park of broken pieces to try to mend a broken world."

After some fifteen years of working on this backyard Eden, Finster had a vision instructing him to create a number of paintings he calls sacred art. A few years later, he built the World's Folk Art Church near the garden to serve as a sort of holy art gallery. Its purpose, said Finster, was to reveal "the truth of God, the truth of mankind and his discoveries, the truth of the present, and the truth of the future."

Raymond Isidore (left) decorated every conceivable object in his house, from flowerpots to the furniture (inset, below), with pieces of broken glass and crockery. The locals dubbed him le pique-assiette—French for sponger, or borrower—and his creation La Maison Picassiette.

A Glittering Mosaic of Broken Glass

"We discard so many things that could be used to create life and happiness," Raymond Isidore once said. He was himself, however, a striking exception to this observation. From 1938 until his death in 1964, the French cemetery caretaker, a resident of Chartres, collected ceramic and glass fragments from dumps, roadsides, and his acquaintances and used them to create the fantastic mosaics that eventually covered every inch of his house and garden (right).

Reportedly inspired by God, nature, and the great cathedral in his town, Isidore embedded both the interior and exterior walls of his home with scenes from the Bible, models of Chartres and other cathedrals, and various images he found pleasing. Isidore believed he was guided by a divine spirit, although he also admitted that he created the monument to suit his own tastes, so that he could live in his own element. His jewel-like house and garden, he said, were a dream come true.

Obsessed with light and reflections, Clarence Schmidt illuminated his home with strings of bulbs and tinsel-wrapped wires (above). In the gardens, he built shrines to his heroes. One series honored U.S. presidents, including George Washington (lower inset); others featured photos of Schmidt himself.

An Incredible Edifice Made from Junk

Visionary artist Clarence Schmidt once described the phantasmagorical homestead he created on a mountainside in Woodstock, New York, as a "hallowed undertaking" that would bring "peace and happiness to this vilely mixed up and war torn world."

Around 1948, Schmidt, a plasterer by trade, began enlarging his mountain cabin. He soon became obsessed by the project, devoting all his time and energy to it. Some twenty years later, the cabin and a large tree nearby had been completely swallowed by a thirty-five-room, seven-story tinderbox of a mansion made from discarded junk—scrap wood, tar, and glass.

Inside, strings of Christmas-tree lights illuminated a maze of passageways and rooms encrusted with mirrors and a dazzling collection of cast-off items—including women's shoes, coffeepots, and artificial flowers. The gardens around the house echoed its contents: Sculptures fashioned from other people's rubbish were placed among the trees and shrubs, hundreds of whose limbs and branches were wrapped in foil to reflect light.

The reclusive artist dubbed the original cabin at the heart of his chaotic creation his Inner Sanctum, where he lived what he called a "ritually cloistered holy existence," dedicated to building a new world "all tenderly wrapped up with mountainous harmony and everlasting peace." Unfortunately—perhaps inevitably—Schmidt's highly combustible dreamland caught fire and burned to the ground in 1968; he died ten years later.

Robert Tatin and his wife, Lise-ron, show off a grinning sculpture he called The Beast Tamer (right). Most of his images— which have been compared to Aztec, Assyrian, Mayan, and Inca art—are deliberately symbolic: The dragon inset at lower right, according to Tatin, represents evil, ego, selfishness, and the other trials one must overcome to attain redemption.

A Frenchman's Philosophical Statement

In 1962, sixty-year-old Robert Tatin, a well-traveled Frenchman who had worked variously as a carpenter, sculptor, and ceramist, bought the ruins of an old farmhouse in Cosse-le-Vivien, France. He and his wife, Liseron, soon set about rebuilding the house, but somewhere along the line the project evolved from a mere domestic renovation into a grandiose architectural statement of Tatin's personal philosophy. He believed that human wisdom and happiness lay in a return to the so-called female qualities of instinct and creativity. Accordingly, many of the cement gates and sculptures he and Liseron built by hand on the property over the next nearly twenty years, such as the Gate of the Moon (below), idolize the female principle. For Tatin, whose creation is now a national museum, art—including his own, no doubt—was "a means for developing the marvels within us."

CHAPTER 2

Seeking Eden in America

leaky old vessel named *Mariah* set sail from Liverpool in May of 1774, bound for New York. On board was a short, stout woman in her thirties named Ann Lee. With brown hair, blue eyes, and a mild expression, she looked more like a schoolmarm than the zealous leader of the religious spiritualists who had boarded with her. They had been hounded out of their native Manchester because of their heretical beliefs. Several months before the voyage, Ann had experienced a dramatic vision. She saw a large tree, whose every leaf shone with a burning light. The tree told Mother Ann to lead her flock into the New World, where they would find salvation. They almost did not get there.

A few days into the voyage, *Mariah*'s captain watched horrified as his passengers performed their Sunday worship. Shaking and trembling, with wild grimaces, they whirled like dervishes, gyrated with outstretched arms, rolled on the deck, danced and sang and cried out in exotic languages of the spirit world. Scandalized, the captain threatened to throw them overboard if they ever repeated their blasphemous proceedings.

Yet on the following Sunday the same ritual occurred. The angry captain summoned his crew and was about to make good his threat when suddenly a violent storm blew up. Very soon the vessel was sorely beset. Springing a plank in her hull, she began to take on more water than all hands at the pumps could control. The captain, so the story goes, "turned pale as a corpse" and declared that the ship and all aboard her must surely perish before dawn. Then Mother Ann went to the captain and reassured him. "There shall not a hair of our heads perish," she prophesied. "We shall all arrive safely in America. I just now saw two bright angels of God standing by the mast, through whom I received this promise."

At that moment, a powerful wave struck the ship with seemingly miraculous aim, knocking the plank back into place and stopping the leak. Soon the storm abated. Mother Lee sailed on to America and her appointment with destiny. Within two years, Lee and her small band had founded the United Society of Believers in Christ's Second Appearing, just as the burning-tree vision had ordered. Better known as the Shakers, they became one of the most successful and long-lived utopian societies founded in the New World.

Scores of utopian groups blossomed in America during the eighteenth and nineteenth centuries. Most withered quickly, but some flourished and became established elements of American society. Besides the Shakers, successful groups included the Harmony Society, the Inspirationists, the Perfectionists, and the transcendentalists. A vivid diversity distinguished these groups, but most shared a peculiarly American amalgam of down-to-earth practicality and mysterious otherworldliness.

The early American utopian groups had deep roots in the Reformation. Led by Martin Luther, this sixteenth-century revolt against the ecclesiastical tyranny of Rome eventually spawned a profusion of Protestant sects characterized by devout scriptural piety and powerful anticlerical prejudice. Many of them were fervent millennialists who believed in the imminence of Christ's Second Coming. After the Savior's reappearance, the sinful would be forever damned and the truly pious would bask in Christ's heavenly grace on earth for a thousand years—the millennium.

The conviction of millennialists would be perhaps most strikingly demonstrated in the mid-nineteenth century, when an itinerant Baptist preacher named William Miller rode to prominence on the notion that the Second Coming was at hand—sometime between March 21, 1843, and March 21, 1844. Expectation was heightened when a large comet showed itself in the February sky. But the year passed uneventfully, so Miller decided to move the date to October 22, 1844. The faithful gathered by the thousands on rooftops and hills and in treetops to await the coming. But, as one writer put it, "the day came. And Christ did not." Miller's failure became known by his followers as the Great Disappointment, but his powerful influence launched the Adventist movement, still a potent religious force in America.

All utopians were convinced that by following their own divinely ordered tenets they could raise the human condition to a near heavenly perfection. By and large they lived in communes securely isolated from the wickedness of the world. They usually had communal economies, wherein everyone expected to share equally not only the physical and spiritual labors that produced their earthly paradise but also the material benefits of those labors. Most of the societies were committed to chastity, and many treated women with far greater equality than found outside. For all of them, honest work was exalted and strict order the rule.

One more factor stands out as a key to the success of utopian societies in America. Almost every one of them was guided in its quest by a charismatic and often mystical leader who claimed direct inspiration from God or Scripture. To a great extent, the success or failure of the utopian societies depended on their leaders' clarity of vision and strength of will, and the essence of the utopian movement can be captured in the chronicles of its leaders.

But why did all those pious, energetic men and women come to America to found their utopias? The answer lies in what the people of Europe heard about the New World in the decades following its discovery. Reports from across the Atlantic pictured America as near an earthly approximation as could be found of the ancient notion of Eden, where primitivism and simplicity were the hallmarks of virtue and happiness, or of Canaan, the land of milk and honey, where God's chosen people would achieve perfection after a long process of self-purification. Furthermore, the New World lay to the west—where the Greeks had placed the fabled lost island of Atlantis and where Sir Thomas More in 1516 positioned his literary vision of a perfect England, to which he gave the name Utopia.

Christopher Columbus promoted the paradisiacal image of America when he portrayed the Indians he found there as innocent primitives, naked as Adam and Eve. He wrote that the air of the New World was filled with the music of nightingales (although in fact that species did not exist in America at the time). Other explorers depicted a land of vast wealth, boundless fertility, and harmonious societies. Such glowing images kindled the imagination of Europeans. Weary of wars, kings, poverty, religious persecution, and plague, they embraced the idea of the New World as a panacea for civilization's ills.

And even though the early emigrants from Europe found a far harsher land than they had imagined, they eagerly took to themselves the mantle of utopia. John Winthrop, governor of the Massachusetts Bay Colony in the early seventeenth century, borrowed the language of Saint Matthew (5:14) to urge the highest Christian behavior on his fellow Puritans: "We must always consider that we shall be a City Upon a Hill—the eyes of all people are upon us." This vision of a radiant New World society seemed a potent au-

Joseph Smith (above) was only fifteen when he said angels first appeared to him and twenty-two when he announced discovery of the golden plates that led to his founding the Mormon faith. His successor, Brigham Young (far right), who led the Mormons on their trek from Nauvoo to the Great Salt Lake (near right), served as first governor of the Utah Territory. But U.S. president James Buchanan removed him from office in 1857 because Young advocated polygamy in the new Zion.

The Mormons' Long Trek to a New Zion

Perhaps the most indefatigable quest for an American utopia was that of the Church of Jesus Christ of Latter-day Saints, formed in 1830 by Joseph Smith. The group's guiding document was the *Book of Mormon*—a supposed translation by Smith of divine wisdom inscribed on golden plates he found near his family's New York farm (and subsequently lost). Thus inspired, the Mormons yearned to build a new holy city, Zion, and await Christ's return.

In search of a site for Zion—which was to be a mixture of Eden and the New Jerusalem described in the book of Revelation—the Mormons made their westward odyssey. From Palmyra, New York, they trekked to Ohio, where financial problems hindered them. Next they tried Missouri, but locals drove them away. In 1838, they settled at last on the Illinois bank of the Mississippi. Smith dubbed the place Nauvoo, saying it meant rest and beauty.

They laid out Nauvoo in two zones prescribed by a "Plat of the City of Zion" that Smith said God had sent him. The sacred zone (Jerusalem) held two huge buildings: the temple—built according to a blueprint from God—and the prophet's residence. The secular zone (Eden) was divided into large blocks, each with four houses and vast gardens. "Let the division fences be lined with peach and mulberry trees," exhorted a local paper, "and the houses surrounded with roses and prairie flowers, and their porches covered with grapevines, and we shall soon have some idea of how Eden looked."

Nauvoo grew to be Illinois's largest city, numbering some 20,000. But although Smith called it "the great Emporium of the West," it never developed much trade or industry, perhaps because neither its sacred area nor the thinly populated residential zone offered a focus for commercial life.

In 1844, Smith was murdered by an anti-Mormon mob. Fearing more violence, the state ordered the Mormons out of Illinois. Under a new leader, Brigham Young, they left their Eden and again journeyed west, eventually founding another Zion next to Utah's Great Salt Lake. Spared the split between the sacred and the secular that had hampered Nauvoo, Salt Lake City became a major metropolis—and, in many ways, a Mormon utopia.

gury of man's perfectibility. In America—boundlessly fruitful and unfettered by clerical tradition or class distinction—anything was possible, even Paradise in the here and now.

This vision of America infused the political and philosophical optimism that eventually produced the Declaration of Independence and the Constitution. It was also inherent in the waves of intense religious revivalism that swept the cities and settlements of America in the 1730s and 1740s, a movement now known as the Great Awakening. Evangelists crisscrossed the colonies spreading the Word and ensuring that religious zeal advanced with the frontier.

William Miller's apocalyptic vision in the middle of the nineteenth century was by no means the first to identify America as the site of Christ's deliverance. A century and a half earlier, a poignant chapter of New World utopianism began when a former Lutheran minister in Germany became convinced that the world was going to end in the autumn of 1694. Johann Jacob Zimmermann, who had forsworn Lutheranism in favor of a strict fundamentalism, was also a devout believer in astrology. His readings of the stars and certain biblical passages led him to believe that Christ would come soon. But where would he appear? Zimmermann sought the answer in the book of Revelation.

From what he read there he determined that the true Church (the only one that would survive the Apocalypse) was symbolized by a woman, who would be given "two wings of an eagle that she might fly into the wilderness." It was clear to Zimmermann that said wilderness was America. Apparently he figured the female image of the Church did not imply that women should participate, because he decided to establish an all-male monastic community in the New World. There celibate monks would purify themselves to meet God face to face.

Zimmermann assembled a band of devoted followers, but on the eve of their departure he died, apparently of natural causes. Undaunted, his band pressed on, now led by a young member, Johannes Kelpius, who shared Zimmermann's fundamentalism and belief in astrology and added his own knowledge of alchemy, Rosicrucianism, and ancient German superstition. The brothers arrived in America on June 19, 1694, and made their way into the Pennsylvania forests, where they founded the community of the Woman in the Wilderness. They built a forty-square-foot wooden tabernacle and took turns sitting on its roof with a telescope, searching the sky for signs of the Apocalypse. Kelpius himself withdrew to a cave.

The year 1694 ended with no sign, but several spiritual manifestations kept their faith alive. While waiting for the end, the brothers carried their gospel to the surrounding countryside and set up a printing press to help spread the Word. Ardent musicians, they published what may have been the first book of music in America. Subscribing to the belief that Native Americans were members of the biblical lost tribes of Israel, they proselytized the Indians and studied their languages to compile a written Indian vocabulary.

Again and again the brothers believed they saw signs that the millennium finally was at hand, and again and again they were disappointed. The best-educated members of the group drifted away. Kelpius refused to question the imminence of the millennium. But when he died from tuberculosis at the age of thirty-five, his brave little church in the wilderness died with him.

Another German pietistic community, the grim Ephrata commune, did better. Founded in Pennsylvania in 1732 by a vigorous mystic named Johann Conrad Beissel, Ephrata (another name for Bethlehem) accepted women, who were known as Spiritual Virgins, but the sexes were rigidly separated. The chapel benches on which the faithful sat for hours of sermonizing by Beissel were uncomfortable to the point of being torturous. The low, narrow doors and corridors in their austere buildings were designed to require normal-size people to bend as they passed, a reminder of the scriptural warning that "narrow is the way that leadeth unto life."

Members retired at nine p.m. but were roused at midnight for an hour of services and again at five a.m. Food

The original of this reconstructed labyrinth of hedges was created at Harmonie, Indiana, by Father George Rapp—seen at about age eighty in the inset. The maze, which contained a small central temple as the goal for those negotiating it, was believed to be a representation of the search for spiritual fulfillment.

was meager and meals were eaten in silence. Field chores usually done by mules were assigned to the brothers. And over all, Beissel ruled supreme. Anyone who disagreed with him in the least detail was branded a sinner and expelled from the community.

Beissel's despotic rule ended with his death in 1768, and within a few years the commune dissolved. But it was not forgotten. Beissel had been a fine musician. Ephrata's choir was renowned and its school highly respected. The community published many books, and Beissel's hymns influenced the course of American hymnology. Today, Ephra-

ta's restored buildings are a popular tourist attraction in Lancaster County.

In 1803, another German evangelist, George Rapp, brought his own millennial utopianism to America. The Rappites, also known as the Harmony Society, adopted a more accommodating relationship with the temporal world, and they fared notably better. Though intensely spiritual, they drank alcohol, ate robustly, and at first, enjoyed their pipes. Eventually, they did give up tobacco.

Born the son of a farmer in Württemberg in 1757, George Rapp started preaching in his home at the age of

married couples considered their bonds dissolved.

Skeptics have since charged that despite his public show of reluctance, Rapp himself pushed for this profound change because his own sex drive had ebbed. Sympathetic observers hold that the community was seeking serenity in order to better prepare for the expected rule of Christ on earth. Twenty years later, an observer described in his diary a conversation with a Rappite schoolmaster: "He told me today that marriage is not forbidden among them, but as they expect Christ to reappear soon, they wish to be prepared to meet him in a fit state, which they could not be if they were taken up by sensual pleasures."

In 1814, the Rappites grew dissatisfied with Pennsylvania, because the soil was uncongenial to the wine grapes they were trying to cultivate. So they moved to the banks of Indiana's Wabash River, where they established another town named Harmonie. Within a few years, fertile fields and rows of grapevines surrounded neat streets, lined with identical brick residences that were forerunners of twentieth-century prefabs. Ready-to-use structural components, including insulation panels, were numbered and stocked in a central warehouse. Strangers used to the slapdash look of most frontier towns were amazed by Harmonie's clean and orderly aspect, and many thought they had indeed stumbled on at least an outpost of utopia.

More Germans arrived to join the Rappites, and at their peak they numbered some 900 souls. So prosperous was their community that they readily agreed that all of its property be held in common. In 1818, they ritually burned the book that recorded the amounts each family had originally brought into the community. Father Rapp was disinclined to recruit new members, and his followers concurred with him. After all, if Christ was soon to reappear, as they

thirty to a small band of followers, who called him Father. Rapp spurned the Lutheran church, denouncing all church authorities as hypocrites. He never doubted that the world would end while he was alive and that he, personally, would present all of his disciples to Christ for their ascension into heaven. Predictably these teachings were regarded as seditious by both Lutheran and civil authorities, and Rapp and his followers were repeatedly jailed as heretics.

But they had an advantage that most other persecuted Nonconformists lacked. Many of the Rappites, including George Rapp himself, were successful farmers and had money with which to leave Germany and establish themselves elsewhere.

In 1803, Rapp sailed for America, where he used his and his followers' funds to buy 5,000 acres of land north of Pittsburgh, Pennsylvania. A year later, some 600 faithful followed and began building the community of Harmonie. They quickly created a large and successful commune, with a number of small industries, including a whiskey distillery. The Rappites loved to eat, putting away four or five large meals a day, and visitors found the portly, congenial group remarkably free of the fanaticism that marked some millennialist communities.

Beneath the placid exterior, however, intense religious feeling burned. In 1807, a wave of fervor swept over the Rappites and a group of them proposed that the community become celibate. Rapp, after expressing reservations, was persuaded to endorse the change. Marriage was not actually forbidden, but sentiment in the community strongly favored total abstention from sex, and the majority of the

fervently believed, why should they worry about the future?

Yet in 1824, Father Rapp, disturbed perhaps that complacency would dim their spiritual fire, enjoined his disciples to move again. They sold their land on the Wabash and returned to Pennsylvania, to a site not far from their original home. Here they established the town of Economy, and here some rumblings of discontent were heard.

There were claims that Father Rapp was selfish and despotic and that he employed shamanistic tricks, such as scurrying back and forth through a secret tunnel to convince his followers he could materialize in two places at the same time. There was even a dark rumor that when his son Johannes married in defiance of the celibacy order, his father had had him castrated and that Johannes had bled to death. The story was never proved, but it is true that Johannes died in 1812, shortly after the birth of a daughter, Gertrude, who then lived with her grandfather.

In 1831, a rival appeared on the scene. A German religious charlatan by the name of Bernhard Müller, who styled himself Count Maximillian de Leon, wheedled his way into the community along with a small band of confederates. Müller recruited dissident Rappites and began pressing Father Rapp to divide the community's wealth. Rapp bought Müller off with a cash settlement that barely affected the now wealthy community's economy, and the group settled down once again.

In 1847, close to ninety years old, Father Rapp died. For thirty more years, Economy remained vigorous, though inhabited only by elderly people. A visitor in 1874 noted that they seemed uninterested in whatever the future might hold apart from the millennium. "The people look for the coming of the Lord; they await the appearance of Christ in the heav-

ens; and their chief aim is to be ready for this great event." None was to see that glorious day in mortal form; the last of the Rappites died in 1921.

George Rapp began his utopia-building enterprise with a ready-made community. That his disciples shared one language and a common national heritage buttressed their cohesive spirit. Ann Lee—she whose vision of bright angels had allegedly calmed the Atlantic storm en route to America—had a harder task. She arrived in New York with only her husband, brother, and five other disciples. She saw herself as a medium between ordinary people and the extraordinary life of the spirit. To build her church, as commanded by the burning-tree vision, she had to start from scratch. Yet within a decade she had launched a movement that has lasted more than 200 years and that at its peak embraced some 4,000 Believers (some estimates range as high as 7,000) in twenty-four different communities scattered from Maine to Indiana to Florida.

Born in 1736 to a poor blacksmith and his wife in Toad Lane, Manchester, England, Ann Lee was an unusually somber child. Early on she told of being visited by religious visions, which convinced her that the world was depraved and wicked. At the age of twenty-five, she reluctantly married Abraham Standerin, a blacksmith like her father, and gave birth in quick succession to four children. All of them died in birth or infancy, a trauma that unquestionably affected her future convictions about celibacy.

When Ann was twenty-three, she joined a small sect that had broken away from

Visitors from the nearby Poland Spring Hotel sit in the back of the hall, behind Shaker worshipers, to observe an 1885 meeting at Sabbathday Lake, Maine. The celibate Shakers welcomed outsiders to their meetings as a way to interest and recruit members. But this picture, taken by a hotel photographer, is the only known photo of a Shaker meeting.

the Quaker faith. The church emphasized a direct spiritual contact between the individual and God, and its form of worship was "ecstatic"—involving the physical gyrations that would later so scandalize the captain of the *Mariah*. Outsiders referred to the sect derisively as the Shaking Quakers, or Shakers.

Life grew perilous for the Shakers as their reputation spread. Their singing, dancing, and shouting worship was deemed a breach of laws protecting the Sabbath, and Shakers frequently were rousted from their services and jailed. Ann Lee, meanwhile, grew increasingly influential within the group, mainly on the basis of her forceful personality and the dramatic intensity of the visions she reported.

In 1770, while in the Manchester jail on a charge of Sabbath breaking, Lee experienced a vision that eclipsed all previous ones. Christ appeared and showed her Adam and Eve engaging in sex. Ann was made to understand that their copulation had been not a natural act for propagation but one of self-indulgence and was therefore sinful—and that this was the act that had brought the Fall of mankind.

Thenceforth, she declared, only persons who forswore all carnal behavior could hope for salvation. Impressed by the power of this insight, members of her sect declared Ann Lee their leader and began calling her Mother Ann and Ann the Word. Eventually her role expanded to render her a female incarnation of Christ's spirit. Not long after came the burning-tree vision that sent her to America.

After the *Mariah* delivered Ann Lee and her little band to New York in the summer of 1774, she stayed in the city while some of the others went up the Hudson River to look for a place to settle. Mother Ann worked as a laundress. Her husband soon disappeared into the bowels of the city, escaping her fiery piety and unilateral vow to eschew sex. She rejoined her cohorts in

Warring Song

Giving

1776, in Niskeyuna, near Albany, and began the work she had come to the New World to accomplish.

She encountered conflicting responses. To Baptist farmers dissatisfied with what many felt was an overly formal church, Ann Lee's exhortations to a more intensely spiritual commitment fell on receptive ears. To Calvinists rendered spiritually powerless by their grim doctrine of predestination, the Shakers' insistence on taking a personal hand in their own salvation seemed to put heaven within reach of anyone. All along the New England frontier Americans began to take notice of Mother Ann.

But there were problems. Shaker worship was undeniably odd, and celibacy, temperance, and renunciation of personal property did not come easily to frontier men and women. Nor did the Shaker concept of God as a dual male-female deity, with Mother Ann as Christ's female spirit, sit well with some. Furthermore, the Shakers' religious convictions would not allow them to take sides in America's war with England or, later, to swear allegiance to the new United States.

These deviations produced a wrath even greater than the sect had known in Manchester. During a missionary tour between 1781 and 1783, Ann Lee and her followers were stoned, kicked, and beaten with clubs. A year later, at the age of forty-eight and greatly

When outsiders began attending Shaker meetings, the wild and impromptu "laboring" that had characterized the Believers' earlier dancing began to evolve into a more orderly ritual. The first distinct dance movement, called the square order shuffle, was introduced in 1785 by the puritanical Shaker leader Father Joseph Meacham, who was inspired by a vision of angels dancing before God. More steps, such as the ones shown by this Shaker sister, were later developed to inspire humility, defeat temptation, and bring about the gifts of spiritual love.

Receiving Love

Quick March

Humility

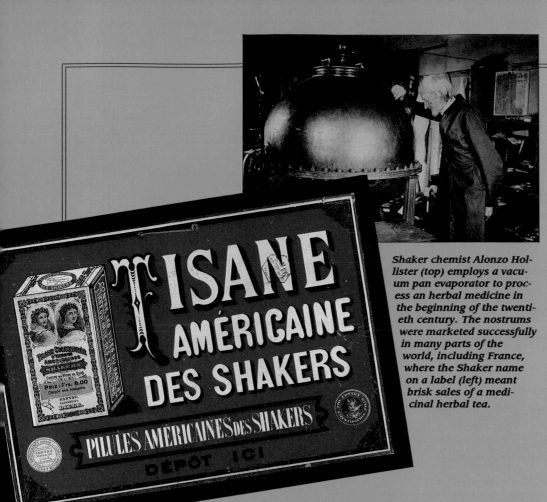

Shaker chemist Alonzo Hollister (top) employs a vacuum pan evaporator to process an herbal medicine in the beginning of the twentieth century. The nostrums were marketed successfully in many parts of the world, including France, where the Shaker name on a label (left) meant brisk sales of a medicinal herbal tea.

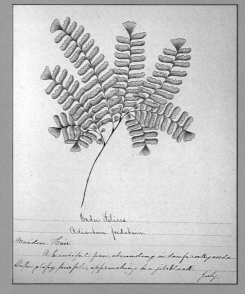

LADY'S-SLIPPER

Considered a "nerve root," Lady's-Slipper was gathered in August or September and used to treat headaches and other mild nervous disorders.

A Shaker Catalog of Herbal Remedies

The Shakers were an enormously industrious and inventive group, ever interested in improving everyday life with new, innovative devices and techniques. They are credited with inventing the flat broom and the circular saw, for example, and with being the first to merchandise garden seeds in paper packets.

The Believers also built a thriving business in the area of herbal medicine. Although they relied mostly upon spiritual healing to relieve diseases, the supernatural gift was considered too precious to be used on all common ailments. Hence, the Shakers turned to herbs as a religiously acceptable means of relief.

Some knowledge of herbs came with them from Europe, but they carefully studied plants and roots shown to them by earlier settlers and American Indians. Despite some unfortunate experiments with poisonous plants, they accrued impressive expertise in growing, gathering, and processing various ingredients for use in their home remedies.

By 1830, the Believers were selling their herbs and extracts to a variety of dealers, drug firms, and doctors—some as far away as Australia. One of the most popular nostrums was the Shaker sarsaparilla syrup. Sold in concentrated form for about one dollar per bottle, it was hailed in an 1847 advertisement as a cure for "Diarrhoea," "Cutaneous Eruptions," and "Headaches of every kind," as well as a host of other maladies.

Salesmen pointed to the well-documented longevity of Shakers as testimony to the effectiveness of their medicines. Although that longevity was probably more attributable to the Believers' temperate, dedicated, low-stress lifestyles, many of their herbs had genuine medicinal effects. But in the wrong doses, some could also be dangerous. None of those shown here should be consumed except on a physician's advice.

MAIDENHAIR

A beautiful fern with a glossy purple stalk, Maidenhair is found in damp, rocky woods. It was used by the Shakers in the relief of coughing, asthma, influenza, and other ailments.

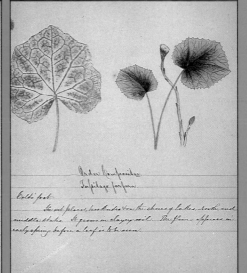

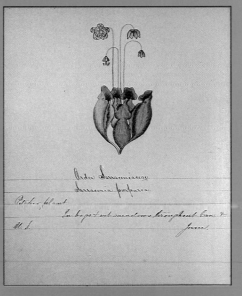

SHEPHERD'S-PURSE

A common weed found abundantly in fields, pastures, and roadways, Shepherd's-Purse was thought useful in controlling scurvy and in stopping hemorrhages.

BAYBERRY

Considered valuable in treating diarrhea and dysentery, Bayberry was also used in powdered form as a snuff to treat nasal congestion. It is usually found in dry woods or in open fields.

COLTSFOOT

Sometimes called Ginger Root or Coughwort, Coltsfoot was used in treating whooping cough and pulmonary disorders. It was also taken in snuff form for headaches or used externally as a poultice.

FALSE HELLEBORE

Used to treat pneumonia, typhoid fever, and itching, False Hellebore was also an insect poison.

SNAKEHEAD

Called Fishmouth and Turtlebloom, among other names, this herb acted as a gentle laxative and as a tonic for the liver.

PITCHER PLANT

Found in bogs and wet meadows throughout Canada and the United States, Pitcher Plant (also called Eve's Cup and Fly Trap) was used in preparing stomach tonics.

A Vibrant Black Spirit

In 1838, some young Shaker women said that on a visit to the "spirit land," they saw white slaveowners serving their former slaves. Shakers nodded in understanding: God was just. Unlike many Americans of the era, they did not bar blacks from their fellowship nor from their dreamed-of utopia. Perhaps the most remarkable black to enjoy this equality was a charismatic Philadelphia woman, Rebecca Jackson.

Jackson was an illiterate thirty-five-year-old seamstress who knew nothing of Shakers when, she said, a spirit taught her to read and write. Thus she could tell her story in a misspelled, unpunctuated but fiercely compelling autobiography. God called her to preach in 1830 during a storm that "was athundering and Lighting as if the heavens and earth Ware a coming to gather." From 1833, she said, a spirit woman showed her how to behave, "how to walk through the world." In 1836, on her first visit to a Shaker community, she realized from their dress and demeanor that her spirit guide was a Shaker. "I had never seen anybody before that looked like her," she wrote. "I loved this people."

Jackson's vivid visions often set her at odds with the world. Her brother, an African Methodist Episcopal church leader, thought her insane. Her husband tried to kill her when she chose celibacy. Her spiritual life was too vigorous to be contained even among Shakers, who routinely traveled into the spirit world. In the 1850s, she got their backing to found in Philadelphia a mostly black society of Shaker sisters whose services were marked by powerful ecstatic visions. One of her followers was Rebecca Perot (right). After Jackson's death in 1871, Perot assumed her mentor's name and the leadership of the group, which remained active for another forty years.

weakened by the abuse, Ann Lee died in Niskeyuna.

Yet although she never saw a single Shaker community, the seed she planted bore fruit under the leadership of Joseph Meacham and Lucy Wright, the church elders who undertook to turn Mother Ann's vision into reality. The number of converts grew, and within ten years of Ann's death, eleven Shaker communities flourished in New York and New England.

Typically, a community comprised several "families" with as many as 100 members each. The villages operated on a system of authoritarian control and carefully planned divisions of labor. Every minute was ordered according to a church plan. Most distractions—from bright colors to musical instruments—were frowned upon, and members were enjoined to avoid contact with the outside world. Job assignments were rotated to relieve monotony, however, and although the women performed the household duties and only men used heavy equipment, other positions were open to both sexes. In all things, the good of the community came first, and thrift, skill, and hard work were especially valued.

Despite all their otherworldliness, Shaker communities carried on a brisk trade as their buckets and baskets, sewn goods, textiles, pincushions, and foods became known "outside." In their business affairs, they made a point of giving good value. As one outsider, the English socialist George Holyoake, put it, "They are the only dealers in America who have known how to make honesty pay.''

The Shakers' reverence for fine craftsmanship was embodied in two of Lee's oft-repeated aphorisms. One was ''Do all your work as though you had a thousand years to live, and as you would if you knew you must die tomorrow.'' The other put her teachings in a nutshell: ''Put your hands to work, and your hearts to God.''

There was never any question that doing God's work was the Shakers' first order of business. Nor was there doubt about where the path to God lay: It was in spiritualism. ''Shakerism was founded in Spiritualism,'' wrote two Shaker eldresses, Anna White and Leila S. Taylor, who collaborated on a book on the subject. ''Its very essence and life principle is that of conscious, continuous action and reaction between the worlds of spirit and of sense. Ann Lee's child life was full of vision and spirit teaching. Her maturity won, through soul agonies almost unthinkable, access into the light of open revelation.''

The center of Shaker belief was Mother Ann's conviction that the millennium already had begun. She taught that Shakers were living halfway between earth and heaven. Proof lay in their ''continuous'' interaction with the spirit world, manifested in the ecstatic dancing and speaking in tongues that was part of their rituals.

These took the form of regular gatherings in the meeting halls at the center of each Shaker village. A meeting on

The Shakers in this wood engraving are participating in one of the twice-yearly imaginary feasts dictated by their faith. The holy gathering took place on the highest ground near each Shaker community, where a sacred hexagonal plot called ''the Fountain'' had been cleared and fenced. The closed rituals and wild dancing were protected by inscribed slabs of marble, which warned nonbelievers away. The Groveland Fountain Stone (left), carved in 1843 by Brother Isaac Newton Youngs, a clockmaker at New Lebanon, New York, is the only such stone still intact.

a ''dancing day'' was described by one of the visitors who over the years observed Shaker behavior. The evening began with the Shakers standing in two ranks, men and women five feet apart and facing each other. The chief elder of the ''family'' in the dwelling stood beween the two lines and delivered a five-minute sermon, concluding by saying, ''Go forth, old men, young men and maidens, and worship God with all their might in the dance.''

At that, the men stripped off their coats and joined the women in a double-time march around the room, while four men and four women remained at the center of the room singing. Soon the men were dancing vigorously on their side of the room and the women on theirs. The dance grew wilder and almost orgiastic in movement, but none of the dancers spoke to or touched anyone of the opposite sex.

When they appeared to tire, the elder gave a signal. The dancers formed an elongated ring, then paused, waiting in silence. Suddenly, two women began to whirl silently across the center of the floor, spinning like tops. The others watched motionless and expressionless. The women whirled for fifteen minutes. Then, just as suddenly, they stopped and returned to their places.

One of the two women said, "I have a communication to make." She mumbled something to the head eldress, who then announced that Mother Ann had communicated with the two whirling women while they danced: "Mother Ann has sent two angels to inform us that a tribe of Indians has been round here two days and want the brothers and sisters to take them in. They are outside the building there, looking in at the windows."

As he could see no one peering through the windows, the visitor was utterly confused until he learned that the "Indians" were spirits who had been dead since before Columbus discovered America. Shortly after this spiritual visitation, the meeting ended. The same visitor was present on a subsequent evening when the Indians were welcomed in by the Shakers: "Whereupon eight or nine sisters became possessed of the spirits of Indian squaws, and about six of the brethren became Indians. Then ensued a regular pow-wow, with whooping and yelling and strange antics, such as would require a Dickens to describe."

Shaker meetings changed over the years, and the dances became more elaborate and formal. But the ecstatic element never disappeared. And in the 1840s, a fierce revival of spiritualism swept the group; it was decreed that twice a year each community should hold a holy feast on a nearby hilltop to reaffirm their commitment to the spiritual world.

Fasting preceded the great day, and in the morning the community trooped to the holy mount in a joyous parade. A description of one such day tells how the Shakers donned spiritual garments of great richness. Each brother was issued, from an imaginary chest, "a coat of twelve different colors; a sky-blue, gold-buttoned jacket . . . a pair of white trousers spangled with stars . . . and a fur hat of a silver color." The women were given similar phantom apparel. Shakers knelt in pairs before the elders and eldresses while two angels bedecked them with splendid imaginary garments.

After much communication with the spirits—at one meeting some 40,000 disembodied souls were said to be present—an elaborate spiritual feast began. Invisible apples, peaches, pineapples, cherries, apricots, grapes, strawberries, whortleberries, pomegranates, oranges, pies, sweetcakes, milk and honey, locusts and wild honey, white wine, and manna (so the records report) were spread on a great imaginary table. The celebrants sat down on real benches to enjoy the banquet, at which great quantities of spiritual wine were consumed—so much that some of the feasters behaved in a decidedly drunken manner.

When the celebration ended, the communicants returned their heavenly costumes. It was said that on one occasion, an elder counting the spiritual garments while packing them away discovered one outfit was missing. An investigation revealed that a sister had gone about her chores forgetting that she still wore her invisible gown.

Such blissful indulgences made up for the sober tenor of the Shakers' daily lives. Mother Ann's strictures on celibacy were unequivocal. Sometimes in worship services men and women exchanged "gifts" of hugs and kisses, but apart from such public occasions, an adult could spend his or her entire life without ever touching a person of the other sex. Women and men ate at separate tables. Buildings had two doors, two stairways, and extrawide passageways so brothers and sisters could pass back and forth without touching. Some Believers could not abide such a regimen and defected to the wicked "outside." Most, though, found serenity in

A Shaker sister has fallen into a trance after spinning like a top in order to communicate with the spirit world in this woodblock print. The ability to receive spirit messages in this manner was known as the whirling gift.

The gracefully curling branches of this Tree of Light, painted by
Hannah Cohoon, represent Mother Ann Lee's seminal vision of a burning tree.
Cohoon, one of the few Shakers to sign works of art, joined the church in
1817 and remained a member until her death forty-seven years later.

A Gallery of Spiritual Visions

During the nineteenth century, certain members of the Shaker faith began expressing their religious feelings and visions through an art form referred to as gift drawings. These curious works, which were generally executed in terms of nature or in elaborate, abstract symbols, are particularly puzzling in light of specific Shaker prohibitions that forbade ornamentation of any sort.

One explanation for the paradox is that Shakers saw the gift drawings not as objects of art but as signs of union with God, much the same as their other "gifts" of songs, dances, and inspired preaching. The individual writings and drawings were, according to Shaker tradition, controlled and dictated by a spirit rather than by a human artist.

There is some evidence, however, of deliberate creation involving the use of ruled lines, a compass, and even preliminary sketches. This suggests that not all "visions" were committed to paper immediately and that they were not necessarily drawn by the same individual who had originally experienced the vision.

Whether the drawings were products of divine inspiration or simply of a brief unfettering of Shaker talent, one thing is certain: They were not greatly prized by the Shakers themselves. Of more than 1,200 thought to have been drawn, only 192 are presently accounted for. The rest were apparently casually discarded.

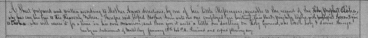

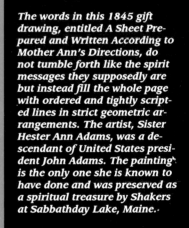

The tree, a favorite motif in Shaker art, is also an apt metaphor for the church members' compelling sense of community. The vision that inspired Hannah Cohoon's ink and watercolor, A Bower of Mulberry Trees (top), came to her during a meeting in 1854. She said, "it was painted upon a large white sheet and held up over the brethren's heads. I saw it very distinctly." Later, the spirit showed her close-up views of painted leaves from the bower "so that I might know how to paint them more correctly."

The words in this 1845 gift drawing, entitled A Sheet Prepared and Written According to Mother Ann's Directions, do not tumble forth like the spirit messages they supposedly are but instead fill the whole page with ordered and tightly scripted lines in strict geometric arrangements. The artist, Sister Hester Ann Adams, was a descendant of United States president John Adams. The painting is the only one she is known to have done and was preserved as a spiritual treasure by Shakers at Sabbathday Lake, Maine.

Unsigned, but attributed to Sister Polly Collins of Hancock, Massachusetts, this ink and watercolor painting, An Emblem of the Heavenly Sphere, honors forty-eight saints of the Shaker faith. Mother Ann Lee, the church founder, is at top left. At the top of the right-hand column is Christopher Columbus; his position in relation to the others demonstrates the importance of the discovery of the New World to the Shaker vision of utopia. Also in the painting are several examples of the Shakers' tree-of-life motif. The inscription describes the joys of "the happy land above."

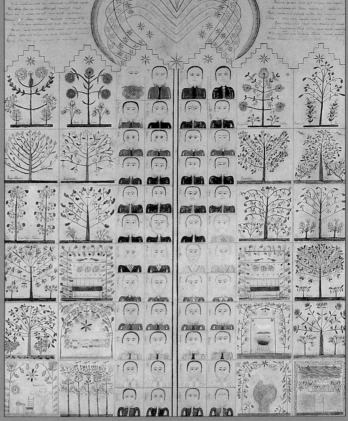

The City of Pease (left) is one of the few gift drawings produced by a male Shaker. Created in 1844 by Elder Joseph Wicker, who was an important "instrument" for spirit manifestations at the Hancock community, the painting is less colorful and more systematic than those painted by Shaker sisters. The links of the golden chain stretched above the tree of life, for example, are plainly labeled with the names of various abstract virtues such as Love, Hope, and Humility. Words written in an unknown mystical language fill the background in geometric shapes.

their enforced celibacy—aided, no doubt, by the strenuous and uninhibited activity of their dances.

Obviously, no children were born to Shakers. But from nearby communities they took in hundreds of youngsters. Some belonged to families joining the movement. Others were orphans. The Shaker villages might well be considered the first orphanages in America, and their schools and communal childcare arrangements ensured that all the youngsters were cared for and taught as well as or better than they would have been in the outer world.

The villages recruited actively among adults in the outside population. The fading of the sect in this century owes less to its zero birthrate than to the decreasing ability of the Shakers to interest new members in a life suspended between the real world and the world of the spirits.

What is left of Shakerism for most of the world today is the remarkable legacy of architecture, furniture, design, and craftsmanship. Mother Ann's prescription for careful craftsmanship manifested itself in every edifice they built. Their circular barns, for example, are among the most efficient structures ever constructed for housing cattle, bringing in hay, and getting out manure. The colors of Shaker buildings were carefully mandated. Barns and service buildings were painted dark colors, deep reds, or tans. Workshops and residential houses were lighter, in creams or yellows. The exterior of the meeting house was always white, and the walls and ceilings inside were of blue-white plaster trimmed in dark blue-green woodwork.

Shakers hung their small pieces of furniture on rows of pegs so the rooms could be swept scrupulously clean ("There is no dirt in Heaven," said Mother Ann). The furniture itself is now prized almost beyond worth by connoisseurs of Americana. In the 1980s, a Shaker chair was auctioned for $80,000—a startling material value for what was intended as an expression of spiritual purity.

In the 1990s, only a handful of Shakers survived, some at Sabbathday Lake, Maine, and others at Canterbury, New Hampshire. Most were old, and all looked upon the materialistic interest in their works as a corruption of Shaker spirit. But however bleak the prospects for utopia, none of them regretted the decision to follow Mother Ann.

At the end of the eighteenth century, another female sect leader rose spectacularly into public prominence, her star briefly as bright as Ann Lee's was to become. Jemima Wilkinson's fame spread throughout New England, and her story sheds a lurid light on the millennialist frenzy that seemed always about to emerge all over America.

Wilkinson called herself the Public Universal Friend and claimed to have died while in a fever-induced coma. In death, her original soul had been transported to heaven, where it stayed. God, meanwhile, installed a new animating force, the Spirit of Life, within her body. The Spirit of Life was to employ Jemima Wilkinson to warn the sinful world that the millennium was at hand.

Wilkinson was a master of the calculated dramatic effect. She approached the hamlets of Rhode Island and Connecticut, where she sought her converts, aboard a white horse and dressed in flowing robes—a tall, beautiful woman in her early twenties, with shining dark hair and piercing black eyes. Behind her, a train of robed attendants followed in twos, silent as ghosts.

She preached only to the best-educated and wealthiest residents of her targeted communities, and her influence on them often was electric. A judge named Potter became so entranced that he built a new wing on his house for her exclusive use and eventually bestowed most of his wealth on her. Significantly, the judge's loyalty did not waver even after Jemima took vows of chastity.

But when her disciples declared that she was actually Jesus Christ, Wilkinson's credibility waned, and she was forced to give up her proselytizing and move to a large property she acquired near Seneca Lake in New York. There, in 1790, she founded the community of Jerusalem.

During their first years there, Wilkinson's followers brought in bumper wheat crops, built a gristmill and sawmill, and started a school. By 1800, some 250 people were living under the sway of the Universal Friend. Over time, however, the Friend's hand grew heavy. She demanded expensive gifts from the community, explaining that "the Friend hath need of these things." She punished doubters by making them wear black hoods for three months at a time or ordering them to tie bells to their coats.

Disillusioned, Judge Potter sued to recover his money, lost the case, and left the Friend to her own devices. She grew sick and old and was depressed by the parade of tourists who came to gape at her. When she died in 1819, the community of Jerusalem broke up rapidly, almost as if its inmates had been granted a reprieve. Some may find it hard not to snicker at Jemima Wilkinson's story, but the disciples who followed her "into the wilderness" to prepare for a new age stayed together for some thirty years, longer than many of the sixty or so such American communities that sprang up in the second half of the nineteenth century.

Two of those attempts to create communal utopias, on the other hand, not only survived but still exist, though in a form so altered as to obscure their fervent evangelical origins. Both began as communal societies and ended up as profitable capitalistic enterprises. Yet they could hardly have been less alike in their beginnings.

One, the Amana Society in Iowa, like so many others, could trace its roots to the rich soil of German pietism. But the name endures today principally as that of a manufacturing enterprise that produces a famous line of household appliances. The other, founded in Oneida, New York, was a strictly American creation whose unique tenets included a prescription for free love. Yet it, too, has a prosperous corporate descendant, one that today is among the country's largest makers of stainless steel and silverplated tableware.

The founders of Amana were members of a German sect called Inspirationists, who believed that God provided divine guidance through a succession of human instruments whose spiritual lineage reached back to the sixteenth century. In the 1840s, they decided that God's instrument was a former carpenter named Christian Metz. Barely five feet tall, Metz was blessed with a voice said to soar half a mile when he preached in the countryside around his home in Neuwied, Prussia. When he announced in his booming voice that God had told him that salvation lay in the West, his neighbors were ready to follow.

Eventually the path led to Iowa, where Metz settled some 800 of his disciples. They named their new utopia Amana, from a verse in the Song of Solomon, "Come with me from Lebanon, my spouse, with me from Lebanon! Look from the top of Amana!" Like other groups, Metz's followers discovered that pooling capital and work was the best way to tame the wilderness. Fired by their zeal, they created in a few years a viable farming and industrial society that would have taken a less orderly community decades to achieve.

The people of Amana grappled with the same issues other utopians faced: They wore uniform clothing to discourage comparisons of rank and encouraged a drab asexual appearance on the part of women in order to damp libidinous energies. Marriage was allowed, but celibacy was more esteemed. Temperance was urged for all, but a certain amount of beer drinking and tobacco smoking took the edge off the repression.

Christian Metz died in 1867. The community continued to flourish and in the 1870s was the largest and richest of any of the American utopias. But gradually its inner spiritual fire cooled. Eventually, Amana grew to resemble other conservative, religious, economically successful communities of the early twentieth century.

In 1932, the Amana Society split apart its religious and industrial activities. The business assets were gathered into the new Amana Society. Shares were distributed among members according to years of service, and economic communalism was replaced by a wage system.

The community founded in Oneida in 1847 was a distinctly American experiment in utopianism that went against the grain of most such enterprises in one key way: It championed sexual conduct that thoroughly shocked conventional nineteenth-century society. Yet the quirky experiment worked remarkably well for nearly thirty-five years,

Like a lordly male lion amid his pride, John Humphrey Noyes is seated here at the center of a mainly female group of Perfectionists, next to a summerhouse on their Oneida, New York, estate. The women's short haircuts and their loose trousers under knee-length skirts, visual symbols of their freedom and equality in the commune, were avant-garde if not scandalous in the late 1860s, when this photo was probably taken. The Oneida Mansion House (bottom) was big enough to comfortably accommodate virtually the entire community, almost 300 people. In the 1851 portrait inset at lower left, Noyes is seen at about the age of forty, a decade after he founded the movement.

until, under growing pressure from scandalized moralists, it eased itself into the American mainstream.

Oneida's leader, John Humphrey Noyes, was the son of a congressman from Vermont and a distant relation of President Rutherford B. Hayes. Noyes was a well-educated man also given to visionary insights. One day in 1833, while reading the Bible, he was suddenly struck by a statement Jesus made to Peter concerning the disciple John: "If I will that he tarry till I come, what is that to thee?" Christ was saying—or hinting—that John might remain alive until the Savior's return, the Second Coming. The verses go on to say that these words started a rumor among the disciples that John had been given immortality.

But in a flash of spiritual illumination, Noyes saw Jesus' words in a new light. Christ was not saying that John would live forever—he was saying that the Second Coming would be much sooner than anyone envisioned. Indeed, declared Noyes, Christ must have returned in AD 70 (why he fixed on that year is not clear), one generation after his crucifixion, when John may have still been alive.

Noyes's revelation convinced him that the world already was divided into the sinless and the damned. He took stock of himself, decided he was one of the sinless, and saw his role clearly: to create a heaven on earth in which men and women could live sinless lives without renouncing the God-given pleasures of the flesh.

A young, vigorous man, Noyes had no doubt that one of those pleasures was sex. So rather than seeking to impose more restrictive rules on sexual activity in order to keep people pure, Noyes sought to turn sexual relations into what he thought they clearly must be among the angels— namely, free and open lovemaking.

Noyes argued that one should associate sexuality with "images of the Garden of Eden . . . and thoughts of purity and chaste affection." He insisted that "to be ashamed of the sexual organs is to be ashamed of God's workmanship." Furthermore, he decried monogamy, insisting that one of the first rules of life in heaven is that there is no marriage. Drawing on the Scriptures, he decreed that among the Per-

Mr. Graham's Ideal Diet

"Man is naturally a fruit and vegetable-eating animal," proclaimed Sylvester Graham, a nineteenth-century reformer who was convinced that, through the correct diet, an individual could attain a kind of personal utopia of health, spiritual as well as bodily.

Meat, alcohol, tea, coffee, spices, and heated foods, he believed, overstimulated the stomach, the body's "grand central organ." Their ingestion caused excitability and unnaturally increased the sex drive. This taxed the nervous system, causing nervous breakdowns, insanity, even early death.

A former Presbyterian minister, Graham preached that a poor diet destroyed self-control and that sickness inevitably followed. To ward off these evils, he prescribed cold baths, outdoor exercise, and a spartan vegetarianism that featured whole-wheat bread and plenty of water. In lectures delivered throughout the Northeast in the 1830s, he tirelessly proclaimed the superiority of his diet to the high-fat tablefare common in his day. Most audiences responded with enthusiasm, and soon Grahamite hotels and boardinghouses sprang up to feed eager customers according to the strictures of his regimen.

Grahamism caught hold among a number of utopian groups, too. Shakers were attracted to the claim that a "bloodless" diet made sexual self-restraint easier. Although abstinence from meat never became mandatory, separate vegetarian tables cropped up in Shaker dining halls. In contrast, the free-love Perfectionists became convinced that purer food would create a purer race. The transcendentalists, like Graham, thought an unhealthful diet resulted from rapid industrial growth and city living.

In the end, orthodox medicine helped squelch his provocative notion that the perfect life depended mostly on the gastrointestinal tract. Graham's own health did not help his case. After a nervous breakdown, he died at fifty-seven—but not before he invented a simple whole-wheat biscuit that he viewed as a near-perfect food and that became his most lasting legacy: the graham cracker.

fectionists, as his followers would call themselves, "every dish is free to every guest."

Yet Noyes also saw a dark side to sex. In the first six years of his marriage, his wife, Harriet, had given birth to five babies, four of whom were stillborn. Noyes was determined to find a way to avoid inflicting such suffering on women by preventing childbirth. His route to a solution was tortuous.

He settled on a demanding form of birth control, *coitus reservatus,* which required a man to exert total self-control during lovemaking. Mastering the art of intercourse without orgasm was a high moral challenge for the male Perfectionist. It was also an essential requirement in Noyes's system of marriage, in which men and women were free to have sex with whomever they wanted, within a complicated scheme of go-betweens and rights of refusal. Thus Noyes hoped to provide free love for his followers while reducing the burdens caused by a high birthrate.

Skeptics scoff that Noyes was a charismatic con man who wanted to be the principal player in a sexual free-for-all. Yet that accusation does not negate the success of his social experiment. Amazingly, his prescription for birth control seems to have worked. For the first two decades of the Oneida community, from 1848 to 1868, only one or two children were born a year in an adult population of well over 200, a very low birthrate for the era.

Moreover, the Perfectionists clearly were happy and productive. Religious feeling infused all their activities. At the huge mansion and surrounding buildings that constituted the Oneida community in New York State, as many as 300 followers lived in remarkable harmony, and several satellite communes flourished in other parts of the Northeast. Ingenious practical arrangements made life comfortable, and the latest technological improvements, such as central

Although Thomas Lake Harris was sixty-three when this picture was taken, his eyes still reveal the commanding presence that made him the undisputed ruler of Fountain Grove. In 1891, to allay charges of promiscuity, he wed close friend Jane Lee Waring (below). Both previous wives died.

Fountain Grove's vineyards annually produced 70,000 gallons of

Sexual Mysticism in the California Sun

Wags have it that God occasionally tilts America and shakes it, making all the nuts roll down to California. It is certainly true that the state—hanging as it does on the continent's western edge, as far toward the sunset as a pioneer could go—has long attracted the mystics and the seekers, the social and spiritual experimenters. Among the first in that tradition was the Brotherhood of the New Life, founded by Thomas Lake Harris.

Once dubbed "America's best-known mystic," Harris was better known for alleged sexual improprieties than for his mystical ideas—although the ideas, supposedly gathered on voyages he made to far-off stars and planets, were startling enough. Other worlds, he declared, are inhabited by beings free of sin, whereas humans are tainted by evil from Oriana, a now-destroyed planet that was once part of the Solar System. The Moon, a remnant of that exploded planet, infects Earth with Oriana's evil spirits. The role of the brotherhood was to spawn a regenerated pure society uniting humans and heavenly beings under the guidance of Harris, "the pivotal man."

The commune had thrived for fourteen years in western New York when in 1875 Harris bought Fountain Grove—400 acres near Santa Rosa—and moved his followers there. The hardworking men and women grew grapes, made wine, printed Harris's endless writings on a steam press, and manufactured almost everything the commune used—because objects made elsewhere might bring bad vibrations to Fountain Grove.

But members took their pleasures, too, and strange enjoyments they were. Normal sex, even between married partners, was generally forbidden. Harris preached that each person was wed to a heavenly counterpart, and earthly sex interfered with that celestial union. Instead, members were said to indulge in "bridal play" with angels and to conduct conversations and games with tiny fairies inhabiting their bodies. Apparently this play produced pleasurable physical sensations, which one woman described as "like sexual intercourse, only infinitely more so."

Despite three earthly marriages, Harris's own true bride was Queen Lily of the Conjugal Angels, who, he said, bore him two children in heaven. But his critics charged that not all the sex at Fountain Grove was celestial, especially not in the prophet's case. They said he sometimes decided his heavenly counterpart had entered the body of a woman, with whom he then could have sex while remaining faithful to Queen Lily. One periodical asserted—offering no proof—that he made love to five different women in a single day.

Scandal may have been the reason Harris moved back to New York after fresh accusations in 1891. The commune waned, and Fountain Grove was finally sold to outsiders in 1934. Meanwhile, Harris—who declared himself to be immortal—died in 1906, although some said he simply assumed a new celestial form.

Pinot Noir, Cabernet, and Zinfandel wines. The manor house with its lily pond (inset) was the setting for many social activities.

steam heating, were adopted as soon as they were available. Defections were rare, and Oneida's economy thrived.

One recruit played a critical role in this matter. In 1848, the community welcomed Sewell Newhouse, a trapper whose fame in the north country was equivalent to that of Davy Crockett in the West. Newhouse was known for making the best steel traps in the nation, using a secret method by which he tempered the trap's spring.

Noyes persuaded Newhouse to share his secret and allow the group to manufacture and sell the traps. By the 1860s, Oneida factories were producing up to 300,000 Newhouse traps a year, selling them all over the world at tremendous profit. Later the community started the manufacture of silverware and enjoyed similar success.

Noyes's fixation on perfecting the human condition led him to initiate an unorthodox experiment in scientific breeding. Perhaps not since Plato's *Republic* had such a revolutionary, utopian idea been so explicitly expressed, let alone practiced. Certain Perfectionist couples, chosen for their physical and intellectual virtues, were allowed to have sex without coitus reservatus. Noyes, as one of the chosen, fathered at least ten of the children born in the following ten years. No conclusive scientific results came out of his stirpiculture program (from *stirps,* Latin for stem or stock), but it is recorded that the Oneida infants had a decidedly lower death rate than children in the outside world.

From the beginning, the Perfectionists' radical sexual behavior drew outraged criticism from the conventional world. During the 1870s, rumors began flying that Noyes was about to be charged with statutory rape because of his so-called first-husband rites, in which he engaged in sex with young girls of the community.

For all his declared preoccupation with spiritual matters, Noyes was an immensely practical man. So he withdrew from Oneida, slipping out one night in 1876 and decamping to Canada. He continued to advise the community from exile, though, and in 1879 suggested that in light of outside society's implacable moral outrage, the Perfectionists should abandon the practice of free love.

They followed his recommendation and blunted hostility from the outside world. But without Noyes's charismatic presence, the spiritual basis of the community melted away, and in 1881, Oneida as a formal commune was disbanded. It had spun off its commercial component as Oneida, Ltd. Stock in the company was divided among the Perfectionists, some of whose descendants are still shareholders today. When Noyes died in Canada in 1886 at the age of seventy-four, his remains were returned to the Oneida cemetery, where his grave was marked with a stone identical in size and style to all others.

Although Noyes's experiments with sexual and familial relationships were decidedly eccentric, at least one of his basic themes was within the mainstream of American intellectual debate: the idea that human beings, under divine guidance, should strive for perfection on earth. The question was where that guidance should come from.

Henry David Thoreau's dispassionate gaze from the daguerreotype at far left reflects little of the fierce enthusiasm for observation and inquiry that marked the transcendentalist philosophy he embraced. His fellow transcendentalist, writer and feminist Margaret Fuller (near left), owed her formidable knowledge and intensity to tutoring by her congressman father, who insisted she complete the same courses expected of young men. Fuller died at age forty with her husband and infant son in a shipwreck off New York's Fire Island.

For many Americans, the answer was not to be found in mainstream churches. Members of numerous European sects had come to the New World for the express purpose of rejecting the established clergy. Some evangelists, like John Humphrey Noyes, had anointed themselves as God's prophets, inspired to lead others to the light. But why, asked the nineteenth-century philosophers, were prophets necessary? Why couldn't Everyman receive God's truth directly? Here was a notion that struck a deep responding chord in the democratic political impulses of America.

A group of intellectuals in Boston and nearby Concord began to gather around a doctrine embodying this ideal. Among them were some whose names would still resonate in the minds of educated people more than a century later: Ralph Waldo Emerson, Henry David Thoreau, Amos Bronson Alcott, Nathaniel Hawthorne, and Elizabeth Palmer Peabody. Their new philosophy came to be called transcendentalism. At the core of their belief was the idea that "man is a rudiment and embryo of God."

The transcendentalists felt that man could be at one with God through strict mental self-discipline and close observation of the natural world, which embodied God. In articulating these themes, thinkers such as Emerson—who sensed in all things a tangible spiritual life and intelligence—came surprisingly close to the lessons Mother Ann Lee had preached to the Shakers.

But the transcendentalists were far removed socially and intellectually from the simple Shakers, and their theories produced far different results. Elizabeth Peabody was a teacher who proposed that the educational practices of the day, based on drill, rote, and discipline, had a dampening effect on children. When the school she operated with Bronson Alcott was closed because of public outcry over this radical theory, she established a Boston bookstore that soon became a regular gathering place for the principal figures in the transcendentalist movement.

There they exchanged ideas, read foreign newspapers, and engaged in the kind of frank talk between men and women that was awkward in the general society. Out of these dialogues grew a conviction that to practice what they preached they should transplant themselves to more agrarian settings. Unfortunately, the transcendentalists proved to be less happy there than they were in Peabody's bookstore.

The best known of their utopian communities was also one of the most short-lived—Brook Farm. Founded in 1841 by George Ripley, a young preacher who had turned away from conservative religious beliefs while at Harvard, Brook Farm strove to serve as a community where "thought would preside over the operations of labor, and labor would contribute to the expansion of thought."

The experience of Nathaniel Hawthorne, who later portrayed the farm in his novel *The Blithedale Romance,* epitomized the project's central flaw—the lamentable truth that great thinkers were not necessarily great farmers. When the young Hawthorne, poor but already enjoying a growing reputation as a writer, joined the farm in its first

This portrait of Ralph Waldo Emerson (near right) no doubt displeased the preeminent transcendentalist, who was seldom satisfied with photographs of himself. He once described the daguerreotype as "the true Republican style of painting . . . the artist stands aside and lets you paint yourself." Elizabeth Palmer Peabody (far right) started something of a club for transcendentalists when she opened her Boston bookstore in the early 1840s. Three early books by her brother-in-law Nathaniel Hawthorne were printed on her press. She is also credited with opening the nation's first kindergarten.

season, his main hope was that he could marry his fiancée and have a place to live with her.

Two days after his arrival, Hawthorne recorded in his diary that "after breakfast, Mr. Ripley put a four-pronged instrument into my hands, which he gave me to understand is called a pitchfork, and he and Mr. Farley being armed with similar weapons, we all three commenced a gallant attack upon a heap of manure."

Two days later, Hawthorne informed his diary with an air of surprise and pleasure, "I have milked a cow." But darker thoughts were beginning to intrude: "I have read no newspaper and hardly remember who is President. . . ."

At the end of the first month, Hawthorne's mood had clouded noticeably. He disliked being apart from his fiancée. And the manure heap was putting him in mind of Dante's Inferno. "That abominable goldmine!" Hawthorne wrote to his fiancée. "Of all hateful places, that is the worst. . . . It is my opinion, dearest, that a man's soul may be buried and perish under a dung-heap or in a furrow of the field, just as well as under a pile of money."

Hawthorne left the farm after its first season, although he loyally returned later as a nonworking guest. Ripley, recognizing that the farm lacked an organizational plan, grew increasingly interested in the thought of Charles Fourier, a French socialist who proposed a worldwide network of utopian communities to be called phalanxes. But rather than infusing Brook Farm with new energy, the principles of Fourierism seemed to exhaust the members altogether. They spent most of their time trying to master minutely detailed rules and ornately complex arrangements of committees.

A visitor who happened to arrive at the farm one day when the pigs had escaped from their pen recorded the confusion. As the phalangists ran around helter-skelter, one of them shouted at him, "Oh! The pigs have got into the cornfield, and I am looking for the Miscellaneous Group to drive them out."

Brook Farm suffered hardships not unknown to other farms—disease, hard weather, a destructive fire. But its occupants had other lives to which they could escape. In 1847, they gave up. George Ripley left a bitter, disappointed man.

That same year, Henry David Thoreau was finishing his own solitary experiment in utopianism at Walden Pond. When he published his findings in *Walden,* he called his first chapter "Economy." It was a key point in the history of American utopian thought. The transcendentalists, whose pantheistic beliefs had diluted the strength of their divine commitment, were now turning away from an interest in religion and devoting themselves to reforming the economy and secular society.

The shift from a religious core to an intellectual base cast a pall on the utopian movement. The demands of communal living—and certainly the demands of farming—evidently required a hotter flame than dispassionate intellectualism was able to provide, and the resolution of the transcendentalists was wearing very thin.

At Fruitlands, a farm community near Concord established by Bronson Alcott in 1843, the communalists decided it was unfair to make horses or oxen pull the plows; they considered it wrong to take milk from a cow or wool from a sheep. Some of them even proposed planting only "aspiring" vegetables—those that grew upward toward heaven—and none that grew

Bronson Alcott, the father of author Louisa May Alcott, strikes a typically serene pose at Orchard House, the family's Concord, Massachusetts, home. A gentle, courteous transcendentalist philosopher and educator, Alcott taught his students through conversation. His methods, however, were not widely accepted, and he was forced out of the profession by 1839 with the closure of his last school. An abolitionist and advocate of women's rights, the self-educated Alcott was described by Thoreau as the sanest man he had ever known.

down, such as potatoes. Bronson Alcott also had the idea that it was virtuous to borrow money from friends and not repay them, because doing so drew out their higher natures.

Fortunately for all of the Alcotts, they were able to put such notions behind them when Bronson's daughter, Louisa May, hit publishing pay dirt with her successful novel, *Little Women*. She also wrote what might well be an epitaph for the transcendentalists' farming ventures: "They said many wise things and did many foolish ones."

But while the transcendentalists' efforts at communal utopianism sputtered, Thoreau spoke for all of them in his eloquent description of the ultimate, intimate utopia that lies within each individual. Only by confronting the fears and fundamental loneliness within themselves can people "come to a hard bottom and rocks in place, which we can call reality and say, This is, and no mistake." Only then, he said, can a person live each moment as if it were eternity and realize that utopia is just where one lives, that "here or nowhere is our heaven."

The measure of success of America's aspiring utopians of the eighteenth and nineteenth centuries is not in how their efforts are judged today but in how they themselves judged them then. And for thousands, utopia was truly at hand. By faithfully serving God's will as it was interpreted by their visionary leaders, they believed they were giving their souls a head start on heaven, even while the spirit was still fettered by earthly flesh. The mysterious power of their faith made utterly real for them what for others may have been only an ethereal vision. A scrap of Shaker verse describes as well as anything both the ineffable joy that rewarded the would-be utopians and the heritage that they left behind: "I have looked on a land where the sun ever beams, / And talked with the angels in mystical dreams; / And though some visions may die in their birth, / They still leave the trail of their glory on earth."

Known as a man of enormous warmth and sympathy, Elbert Hubbard (above) suffered through a painfully public divorce from his wife Bertha in 1904 in order to marry his longtime lover Alice Moore (left), who had already borne him a daughter. The second Mrs. Hubbard, a feminist and schoolteacher, died with Elbert aboard the Lusitania on May 7, 1915. A survivor remembered Hubbard saluting the departing lifeboats from the deck of the doomed ship.

A Utopia Built on Commerce and Craftsmanship

It is an irony and perhaps a comment on national character that the one who did most to establish in America the English-born arts and crafts movement—with its respect for the handiwork of rustic villagers—was a slick salesman who made a fortune peddling soap with promotional gimmicks.

Elbert Green Hubbard invented the sales premium, luring customers to Larkin's Creme Oatmeal Soap with free neckties, coffee spoons, baby rattles, and even desks and lamps. He was so successful that when he decided in 1893 to try enterprises he considered more intellectually worthy, he was able to sell his share of the company for a handsome $75,000.

Visiting England in 1894, he met artist William Morris and swooned over the brand of utopianism espoused by Morris, essayist John Ruskin, and others who looked to the romanticized, preindustrial past for their ideals. Inspired by Morris's Kelmscott Press, Hubbard returned to East Aurora in western New York and founded the Roycroft Printing Shop, named for an English printing family of the 1500s.

Adopting the motto, Not How Cheap but How Good, he began producing fine books on a hand press, with handmade paper and illuminations hand painted "after the manner of the Venetian monks." He sold books as successfully as soap: A copy of sonnets he sent to Queen Victoria elicited a note of gushing praise from the monarch, which did not remain a secret.

Before long, Roycroft added new buildings, including an inn, stone and timber cottages, and monastery-like work halls with beamed ceilings. Crafts workers and artists, eventually numbering more than 500, created new products: furniture, stained glass, wrought iron, and leather bookends. A monthly magazine—named, with the reverse snobbery Hubbard loved, *The Philistine*—drew 225,000 subscribers.

A series of "Unconventional Conventions for Immortals and Philistines" attracted to Roycroft such notables as Theodore Roosevelt, Ellen Terry, and Henry Ford. Hubbard became a celebrity himself and hit the lecture circuit, charging $50 extra if the sponsoring group wanted to entertain him.

Hubbard not only wished to create finely crafted articles, he also declared it his purpose to provide satisfying jobs for countryfolk, to prevent their leaving for unhappy lives in the cities. "It's not so much what a man gets in money wages," he said, "but what he gets in terms of life and living that counts."

Critics have alleged that his sympathy was actually with bosses, not workers. One called him "a major spokesman for corporate capital." Corporate capital certainly embraced him. Meatpacking magnates bought a million copies of an article he wrote ridiculing Upton Sinclair's exposé of their industry, *The Jungle.* And reprints of "A Message to Garcia," a famous essay Hubbard penned in praise of those who unquestioningly obey the boss's orders, was distributed in the millions by big companies.

Hubbard, who died in the sinking of the *Lusitania* in 1915, once confessed that Roycroft "began as a joke" but "soon resolved itself into a commercial institution." Yet perhaps a utopian dream survived beneath the commercial exterior: Although the Depression closed the place in 1938, adherents of the Roycroft ideal successfully revived it decades later as a crafts center.

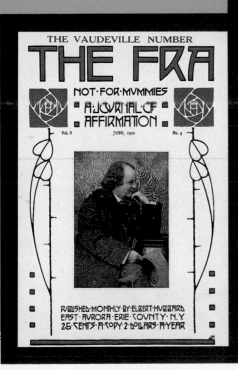

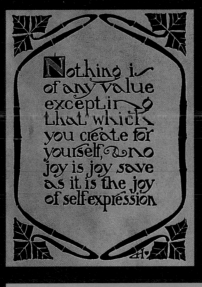

The Fra (far left), more sophisticated than Hubbard's older magazine The Philistine, was launched in 1908 but never reached as wide an audience as The Philistine. Both journals, as well as countless epigrams written and published by Hubbard, like the one at near left, bore the designs of artist Dard Hunter, who created a distinctive Roycroft look.

Dream City by the Sea

I thought as a child that I could fashion a city," wrote the utopian visionary Katherine Tingley, "and bring the people of all countries together and have the youth taught how to live, and how to become true and strong and noble, and forceful warriors for humanity."

From 1897 to 1942, Tingley and her followers strove to realize this dream. On a bluff overlooking San Diego Bay, they launched the Point Loma Universal Brotherhood and Theosophical Society, perhaps the modern age's most ambitious utopian community. At its peak, around 1910, Point Loma housed some 500 members, ranging from infants and children to leaders of industry.

Those who lived at Point Loma were believers in Theosophy—meaning "divine wisdom"—an ancient system of thought that relies on mystical insight to obtain knowledge of God and the universe. The modern Theosophical movement originated in the United States in 1875 under the leadership of a Ukrainian-born Spiritualist, Madame Helena Petrovna Blavatsky. After Madame Blavatsky's death, Tingley broke away to form her own society, headquartered in "the golden land" of California. Under her firm hand, the cherished principles of Theosophy were tested daily.

In time, the community would splinter apart, surviving only thirteen years after Tingley's death following an automobile accident in 1929. For more than four decades, however, Tingley's idyllic inspiration saw glorious life as Point Loma endeavored to lead the world toward a "Universal Brotherhood of Humanity."

A warrior mounts the path to spiritual awareness in this picture from a Point Loma magazine.

Point Loma's Mystical Beginnings

Point Loma was, quite literally, Katherine Tingley's vision. She selected the location sight unseen, as if guided by divine inspiration, and directed its purchase with a steely determination that brooked no earthly interference.

Tingley had resolved to build her city as far west as possible on American soil, symbolizing her emphasis on the Western way of Theosophy. Although she had never actually set foot there, Point Loma, on an arm of land embracing San Diego Bay, proved ideal.

Tingley laid the plans for the community while on a worldwide Theosophical crusade in 1896. After a spirited convention in Dublin, Ireland, she traveled to Killarney to find a cornerstone for the eagerly anticipated Point Loma groundbreaking. Here again, Tingley appeared to receive spiritual insight. She sketched a crude map on the back of an envelope; when her followers reached the spot she indicated, they uncovered a large stone of a peculiar greenish cast, exactly as Tingley had predicted.

Later, Tingley picked up additional cornerstones in Holland and Austria, inspiring her admirers around the world to do the same. Such was Tingley's magnetism that when she returned to the United States for the groundbreaking, eighty cornerstones had arrived at Point Loma.

The stout, vigorous Tingley was sometimes called Point Loma's Purple Mother because of her fondness for that color. Shown here in her forties, she presided over the community for thirty-two years.

Under a banner reading, "There is no religion higher than truth," Katherine Tingley anoints a cornerstone with corn kernels, oil, and wine at the Point Loma groundbreaking on February 23, 1897. Tingley proclaimed the stone "a fitting emblem of the perfect work that will be done in the temple for the benefit of humanity." Nearly a thousand San Diegans attended the ceremonies, which included a dozen speeches, as well as readings from the Bible, the Bhagavad-Gita, and the essays of Emerson. Tingley herself declared that Point Loma would henceforth serve as "a light to lighten the dark places of earth."

A Busy Life beneath the Sparkling Domes

Eventually encompassing 500 acres and boasting a magnificent view of San Diego Bay, the site chosen for the Theosophical community was made even more imposing by the erection of two exotically designed buildings—the three-story Homestead (later known as the Raja Yoga Academy) and the circular Temple of Peace. Both were crowned with huge domes of aquamarine and purple glass. The domes were topped by ornamental glass spheres crested with flaming hearts of glass. During the day, the domes sparkled under the California sun; at night, illuminated from within, they could be seen for miles at sea.

Daily life at Point Loma was busy and full of ritual. Mornings began with a sunrise ceremony and readings from ancient religious and philosophical texts. Katherine Tingley usually offered a few inspirational words of her own as well. After a communal breakfast, which included fresh foods from Point Loma's vegetable gardens, fruit orchards, and dairy farm, the residents went about their tasks. For some, this meant tending to the gardens or to other agricultural ventures such as the bee and silkworm farms. Many women worked in the Woman's Exchange and Mart, where they learned a variety of crafts, including the ancient East Indian art of batik. The men labored in the industrial center, which housed carpentry and machine shops and workrooms for printing, photography, and engraving. Men and women worked together in the book bindery. (Point Loma was known for its printing, winning an international award for printing and graphic arts in 1914.)

Many craft items, from decorated china to fancy leatherwork and doll furniture made of silkworm cocoons, were sold to tourists. Profits from these sales, however, were modest. To keep Point Loma solvent, Tingley re-lied primarily on dues and fees paid by members of the Theosophical Society, and on the generosity of a small but wealthy group of businessmen.

One of these was Albert G. Spalding, a professional baseball pitcher who built a considerable fortune in sporting goods during the early 1900s. Spalding and his wife, Katherine, were so taken by Tingley's Theosophical experiment that they constructed a mansion at Point Loma—complete with a glass dome and an exterior spiral staircase leading to the roof.

Tingley's other supporters included Francis Pierce, head of a New York engineering firm; diamond broker E. August Neresheimer; and Clark Thurston of the American Screw Company. When asked why Tingley held such fascination for these men, Thurston replied: Tingley possessed more business sense "than all of us together."

Point Loma residents gather for an evening meeting beneath the massive glass dome of the Homestead rotunda. The building boasted four glass domes in all; their aquamarine hue was said to have occult significance.

The skyline of Point Loma was dominated by the glass-domed Homestead (at right below) and Temple of Peace (to the left of the Homestead). The settlement also included office buildings, private and communal homes, and circular white cottages for schoolchildren. Residents heading for the Greek theater passed through the big post-and-lintel gate shown in the foreground. At its peak, the community attracted 100 tourists a day, most drawn by the plays, concerts, and seasonal celebrations, such as the May Day festivities shown below.

A Fount of Reformist Fervor

A dedicated philanthropist, Katherine Tingley directed the energies of her Theosophical community toward several humanitarian causes. In 1911, she announced a plan to build Theosophical hospitals for convicts, places where prisoners would be treated as "invalids who had come home to rest," and where, supposedly, they would be "cured" of their antisocial behavior. Despite Tingley's obvious commitment, a lack of financial support forced her to abandon the project.

She and her followers had more success with their efforts to eliminate the death penalty. In 1914, she joined the governor of Arizona in an anti-capital-punishment crusade, accompanying him on a speaking tour of Arizona's principal cities and towns. As a result, the death penalty was abolished in Arizona, though only for a few years. Despite her best efforts, Tingley was never able to repeat her Arizona success in California, although she and her followers often interceded on behalf of prisoners sentenced to die and in one instance persuaded the state to commute the death sentence of a retarded seventeen-year-old boy.

The reform movement that claimed the greatest amount of Tingley's time and energies, however, was her campaign for world peace. Universal brotherhood was a central tenet of Tingley's

brand of Theosophy; indeed, she had added the phrase to the Theosophical Society's name when she became leader of its American branch. For Theosophists, world peace was seen as the natural evolutionary goal of humanity. "In the splendor of a perfect day, brother shall meet brother, soul shall greet soul, and all humanity shall be united, and there shall be PEACE! PEACE! PEACE!," proclaimed one Point Loma publication with characteristic flourish.

Tingley's major campaign for the pacifist cause began in 1913 when she convened an international peace conference in Sweden. A year later, undaunted by the outbreak of war in Europe and the growing signs of America's own war preparedness, Tingley sent a telegram to President Woodrow Wilson, asking him to declare September 28, 1914, as the "Sacred Peace Day for the Nations." Although Wilson gently turned her down, the mayor of San Diego acquiesced, and on the appointed day, the people of that city were treated to a Tingley-organized peace festival that included a spectacular parade led by 600 marines and their marching band.

Representing characters from a Scandinavian peace legend, Point Loma residents march through the streets of San Diego in 1914 as part of a peace celebration organized by Katherine Tingley.

To underscore Point Loma's quest for global unity, its temple (below) was called the Memorial Temple of Peace. Within its ivy-covered walls, gatherings were held to promote Point Loma's striving for universal brotherhood. The 1923 Permanent Peace Congress is pictured above, with Katherine Tingley (center of photo) presiding.

Teachers and children at the raja-yoga school lived together in spotless circular cottages like these (above). Each cottage had a central living room surrounded by bed cubicles and a bathroom and washing area. After 1904, the cottages housed only groups of boys; the girls were moved into the nearby Homestead building, which was then renamed the Raja Yoga Academy. A major part of the raja-yoga educational experience involved participating in pageants and plays. Below, a group of students perform the Highland Fling.

An Education of a Spiritual Nature

Katherine Tingley's most significant undertaking at Point Loma was her raja-yoga school. The name came from a Sanskrit term meaning "royal union"—a title fitting for a school whose mission was to help students find "the perfect balance of all the faculties, physical, mental, and spiritual."

The school opened in 1900 with five students but steadily grew, with an enrollment of 300 a decade later. At one point, more than a dozen nationalities were represented; some students came from such distant lands as Japan and South Africa. Children from wealthy families paid yearly tuition fees of up to $1,000; however, many students, including a large contingent from Cuba, attended the school on full scholarships.

Raja-yoga children were divided into groups of six to twelve, according to age and abilities. Each group was assigned a teacher who supervised the children day and night. All the children shared living quarters with their teachers, even those whose parents lived at Point Loma. Children could see their parents for only two hours—on Sunday afternoons. Tingley may have drawn the inspiration from the utopian model of Plato's *Republic*.

Although the raja-yoga students spent no more than three hours each day in formal classroom instruction, outside educators who visited the school were impressed by the students' academic abilities. "We have come, we have seen, and we are conquered!" declared the California superintendent of schools after a visit to Point Loma in 1906; some raja-yoga teaching methods were later adopted by the California public schools.

When not in the classroom, raja-yoga students spent many hours outdoors, working in the community's gardens or playing supervised games of baseball, volleyball, basketball, and tennis. They also practiced their musical instruments and participated in Point Loma's dramatic presentations.

Corporal punishment was not permitted at the school. Teachers were instructed to discipline the children by appealing to their higher, or spiritual, natures. When children became insolent, they were shown their faces in a mirror and told to smile so that their good nature would return. And although splashing a little cold water on a child's face was thought to deflect tantrums, one teacher who overturned a full bucket onto a pupil's head found herself dismissed. Indeed, the word *punishment* was never used; teachers gave "reminders," which sometimes meant taking away a privilege.

Through all activities—both inside and outside the classroom—the children were expected to maintain a "rule of silence." This meant no idle chatter or gossiping. The rule of silence was Katherine Tingley's invention. She believed silence fed the soul. Adults at Point Loma were also expected to hold to the rule, although it was abandoned with apparent relief after Tingley's death in 1929.

A group of raja-yoga students, ages four to six, begin their formal training in music under the eye of an instructor. Each child was expected to study a musical instrument. In 1905, the students formed Point Loma's first orchestra.

Finding Harmony in the Arts

Music and drama were woven into the fabric of daily life at Point Loma. Katherine Tingley used the arts to teach the Theosophical way of life. "The secret of Life," wrote one Point Loma resident, "is the establishment in ourselves of a reign of harmony, law, and order: and music and the other arts serve as helps and reminders."

To pursue that goal, Tingley created the Isis League of Music and Drama. In 1898, the league produced its first play, the ancient Greek tragedy *Eumenides*, in New York City's Carnegie Lyceum. The performance, which featured a cast of 200, received favorable reviews and was repeated during an international Theosophical convention. "Dramatic work is now the most important activity" at Point Loma, an enthusiastic Tingley proclaimed, "for by its means the minds of men are being gradually permeated by the fundamental ideas of Brotherhood."

In 1901, an open-air Greek theater was built at Point Loma, the first in the United States. Seating 2,500 people and offering a spectacular view of the Pacific, the theater became the center of Point Loma's dramatic productions. Shakespearean plays were added to the league's repertoire, for they, like the Greek plays, were thought to embody grand Theosophical themes, such as the duality of human nature and the quest for harmony. One production, *A Midsummer Night's Dream*, was so popular in San Diego that a train was hired and the entire cast of 150 journeyed to Los Angeles.

The Isis League also introduced the an-

cient Greek cultural tradition of the symposium to its audiences. As time went on, the symposiums grew more elaborate, climaxing in 1911 with a production called *The Aroma of Athens*, which consisted of imaginary discourses between Euripides, Pericles, and other Greek philosophers on "the true, the good and the beautiful."

Point Loma's musical endeavors were equally ambitious. By 1913, the community had two orchestras, a brass band, and several choral groups. Music, frequently in the form of songs and dances, was part of every pageant and celebration. Tingley even opened her speaking engagements with music. Musical notables who visited Point Loma, such as the great Australian opera star Dame Nellie Melba, were often quite exuberant with their praise for the musicians. After a 1916 concert by raja-yoga students, Dame Melba wept with joy and exclaimed, "I have never felt this way but once before in my life, and that was when I heard *Parsifal* for the first time."

Wearing a white robe and garlands of flowers, a raja-yoga student beguiles an audience with harp music before a Theosophical lecture by Katherine Tingley.

Using the dramatic natural setting of Point Loma's Greek theater to great effect, a group of torchbearers march toward the stage during the climax of The Aroma of Athens, a pageant-symposium staged at Point Loma in 1911. Another popular production at the theater was A Midsummer Night's Dream (inset below), in which even the very youngest raja-yoga students, dressed as fairies, danced and sang.

CHAPTER 3

Perfecting the Human Spirit

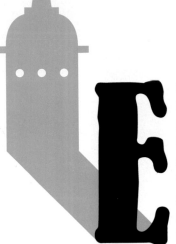

English physician Kenneth Walker was not new to the teachings of Georgei Ivanovitch Gurdjieff when he journeyed to Paris in 1948 to seek instruction from the sage. On the contrary, he had devoted nearly twenty years to unlocking his physical, mental, and spiritual potentialities through Gurdjieff's system of meditation, sacred dance, and self-observation. But the whole of Walker's training had been at the hands of a Russian-born Gurdjieff disciple named Peter Ouspensky, who had parted ways with the master many years earlier. Now Ouspensky was dead and—at his widow's urging—a number of his followers were flocking to Gurdjieff's side.

Walker arrived in France elated at the prospect of finally seeing Gurdjieff for himself. He was also, he admitted, a little apprehensive, because the Gurdjieff legends he had heard over the years had painted a rather befuddling picture. On the matter of age, for instance, Gurdjieff seemed every bit as evanescent as the medieval alchemists of folklore. Some accounts had him pegged at eighty years old; others suggested that he might count his years in the hundreds. And while the master was generally described as wise and charismatic, he was also said to be utterly unpredictable and given to confrontational scenes with his disciples.

The Englishman's misgivings were only made worse by the advice of his colleagues who had preceded him in coming to France. Before escorting Walker to Gurdjieff's flat, they warned him about some of the more eccentric aspects of life in the master's company. They told him, for example, that he would be asked to declare what sort of idiot he was. Gurdjieff, it seemed, subscribed to an obscure Babylonian system for classifying people according to types—twenty-three types in all. Rather than referring to the formal categories, however, he liked to speak of the various kinds of idiots in the world. He taught that the original meaning of *idiot* was ''one's own,'' and he found it useful to have his students assess themselves in terms of this unflattering characterization.

Gurdjieff's drinking habits were another matter about which Walker was forewarned, and since he rarely indulged in alcohol himself, the stories of inebriation caused him much consternation. He was informed, nevertheless, that drunkenness was all but mandatory when sharing lunch or dinner with Gurdjieff. At the feasts the master hosted for his disciples, participants chose either brandy or peppered vodka and joined their leader in a series of ritual toasts to every sort of idiot in the room. Gurdjieff apparently loved to drink and he appreciated the effects of alcohol on the others, claiming that their intoxication allowed him to peer into their hearts.

As Walker was soon to discover, no amount of briefing from his comrades could have adequately prepared him for sitting, conversing, eating, and drinking with his newly adopted guru.

When he was finally led to the old man's quarters, he entered a wonderland of chaos. There was such a bewildering jumble of mismatched paintings and furnishings that Walker had the impression that nothing in the place had ever transpired by design. The flat was hot as an oven, and a strong odor of spices permeated every room. All the curtains were drawn and the artificial light was so jarringly unpleasant that Walker could only guess that the effect was intentional.

Looking back, Walker later would conclude that Gurdjieff wanted the ambiance of his surroundings to be so obtrusive that it would disorient visitors and blot out any thoughts of other places. But at the moment there was no time for such musings. Walker was swept into a large sitting room that was soon jammed to capacity. And with the master nowhere to be seen, a member of the assembly stepped forward to read from one of Gurdjieff's books.

The work was called *Beelzebub's Tales to His Grandson* and—as near as Walker could discern—it was an allegory revolving around the character of the fallen angel Beelzebub. Along with his favorite grandson, this powerful spirit zoomed around the solar system in a spaceship, stopping occasionally to visit the various planets. When the grandson became intrigued by the behavior of the inhabitants of Earth, Beelzebub recounted the history of the human race. What he had to say was not flattering in the least. Gurdjieff would later explain that his purpose in the work was to annihilate all romantic misconceptions about the values and ideas of the past.

About an hour into the recitation, a mirthful-looking man with a bald head and a heavy mustache slipped into the room, and Walker realized at once that it must be Gurdjieff. He watched with fascination as the old man settled in to follow the reading, patiently at first and

Peter Ouspensky (above), who popularized the work of Georgei Gurdjieff (left), also wrote influential books on the fourth dimension and on yogic practice. Ouspensky's teachings were summarized in five or six written lectures, which were read aloud to new pupils before he met them.

Off to the United States in 1924 for a theatrical tour, Greco-Armenian sage Georgei Gurdjieff waves farewell with a characteristic air of benign dignity. The forty students accompanying him put on an eclectic show of ritual dance, magic tricks, and athletic feats.

later with growing agitation. Finally, Gurdjieff interrupted the reader and, patting his stomach, said: "Le Patron is demanding instant attention." With this, he invited the entire gathering to join him for lunch.

When Gurdjieff's guests—numbering several dozen—had wedged into a small dining room, platter after platter of food began to arrive from the kitchen. Among the riches that soon crowded the tabletops were pigeons stewed in grape leaves, pilaf, strawberries in cream, sweetmeats, melons, avocados, and a great variety of other fruits and vegetables. Before taking a bite, however, everyone watched as Gurdjieff labored over one final dish. In a large bowl he mixed fragments of dried fish, bread, pickles, red peppers, cucumbers, onions, many different kinds of chutney, and heaping spoonfuls of sour cream. When he had seasoned this concoction to his satisfaction, he passed the bowl to his nearest companion and the meal was allowed to begin.

From time to time, Gurdjieff would reach out his spoon and offer a choice morsel of smoked sturgeon or some other delicacy to the newcomer Walker. Gurdjieff chided him for eating like a finicky Englishman and made an effort to draw him into the conversation.

For his part, Walker found the old man most extraordinary. He was struck by Gurdjieff's singular way of expressing himself—a free-form mixture of English, French, and Russian so impenetrable to most listeners that an interpreter was kept busy throughout the meal. Even more perplexing was Gurdjieff's habit of shifting moods as he spoke to different people at the table. He could be angry or critical one moment, then relaxed and pleasant the next, only to turn harsh again in an instant. He seemed to read the hearts of those around him and could, like an actor, create any impression he wanted. Gurdjieff was also quick to curse his disciples or to lambaste them for their personal foibles.

True to Walker's worst fears, the meal was punctuated by formal toasts. There were thirteen toasts at least, before Walker lost count, and he found that it was all he could do to remain upright. Mercifully, coffee and cigarettes appeared at last and, without further ceremony, Gurdjieff brought the session to a close—by inviting everyone to dinner. "The reading," he said, "will begin at half-past nine. Now I advise you to lie down and rest for a little, first on your left side and then on the right."

In the days and weeks that followed, Walker fell into the peculiar pace of life under Gurdjieff's tutelage. There were readings at midday and in the evenings, lunch at two in the afternoon, and dinner after midnight. Always the eating and drinking were prodigious. Occasionally, there were quiet breakfasts as well. These were held in Gurdjieff's study, a room that doubled as the pantry and thus was filled to overflowing with groceries.

Walker never lost his sense that Gurdjieff was a mysterious and contradictory individual. The old man seemed unwilling to let anyone around him feel comfortable or complacent for more than a few moments. Gurdjieff's function, Walker concluded, was not to soothe but to disturb. Walker believed, nevertheless, that Gurdjieff was a teacher of immense importance. He came to think of his guru as a link between the twentieth century and the most ancient forms of wisdom. Somehow, Gurdjieff's assault on the mind and the senses—his overindulgence in food and drink, his musings on the follies of the modern age, his unsettling blend of mockery and generosity—convinced followers like Kenneth Walker that they could make a better world.

Utopian philosophy had taken on a new dimension at the beginning of the twentieth century. Georgei Gurdjieff and another energetic critic of conventional Western values—Austrian intellectual Rudolf Steiner—had notions of utopia that had little to do with the religious mysticism of the Shakers and the Rappites or the idealism of the transcendentalists. Neither man placed any great hope in prescribing how societies ought to be structured. And they were equally uninterested in establishing communities apart from the larger society. They emphasized instead the importance of hidden, spiritual aspects of human existence, believing that if thoughtful people could be made to rediscover their

spiritual powers, an enlightened society would follow.

Both men were near the peak of their powers at the turn of the twentieth century. But it is difficult to imagine two more different lives. Gurdjieff wandered incessantly, rarely staying in one place for more than a few months. Steiner's life, by contrast, was quiet and contemplative. Although he left his mark in such diverse areas as philosophy, education, architecture, and dance, he rarely strayed from the libraries and lecture halls of Germany. He taught what he called anthroposophy—his theory of human spirituality and its relation to everyday life. The word, from the roots *anthropos* for man and *sophia* for wisdom, reflected his conviction that humans had spiritual connections to long-forgotten cosmic truths. This neglected wisdom, Steiner believed, could be rediscovered and made a part of everyday consciousness, bringing enormous benefits to society.

Both Steiner and Gurdjieff set out to awaken humanity from what they regarded as spiritual somnambulism. They were deeply influenced by the teachings of the Orient and the ancients, yet they were also enthralled by the legacy of Christ and by modern science. Both taught what they called esoteric Christianity and at the same time embraced the discoveries of physics, chemistry, and engineering. From science they fully expected verification of their spiritual insights. Steiner called his philosophy the science of spirit; Gurdjieff's approach became known as the Work. Their followers thought of both men as heralds of a new age.

Just when that new age began—or will begin—has never been a matter of consensus. For Rudolf Steiner, it began at the turn of the century. According to certain ancient Indian philosophies that he found persuasive, the year 1899 marked the end of the *Kali Yuga,* a 5,000-year-long dark age during which humankind's spiritual faculties had declined to the point where they had all but withered away. The coming cycle was to be an age filled with light. Gurdjieff regarded his own life and teaching as integral to a gradual transformation of the world. The New Age movement that exists today welcomes all sorts of people—from buttoned-down bankers and nuclear physicists to communards forg-

Frank Lloyd Wright's "Shining Brow"

Married to a former student of Georgei Gurdjieff's, the American architect Frank Lloyd Wright *(left)* was himself something of a utopian visionary. "The architect must be master not only of his tools, but of the human spirit," he once told a group of students. "The soul of humanity is in his charge." In his work, Wright tried to guide the human spirit back to its natural origins with "organic" buildings that seemed to grow out of the American terrain.

Taliesin East *(above)*, which Wright intended as a center of American architectural study, is typical of the architect's approach. Of the hilltop building, located near his hometown of Richland Center, Wisconsin, Wright later commented: "Unthinkable to me that any house should be put *on* that beloved hill. It should be *of* the hill.

Belonging to it. Hill and house should live together, each the happier for the other." Wright even selected the name Taliesin—Welsh for Shining Brow—to reflect this relationship between the building and its setting. Taliesin's pagoda-style eaves and ornamental Buddha *(above)* were a tribute to Japanese architecture, which Wright found exceptionally harmonious with nature.

But nature was not the only uplifting influence at Taliesin East. Wright's wife, Olgivanna, gave life at Taliesin a distinctly Gurdjieffian tone. Under her supervision, Wright's students—dubbed the Fellowship—labored with their hands, danced, wove, sang, and painted. At Olgivanna's instigation they even dressed in loose-fitting garments similar to those she had worn for Gurdjieff's sacred dances.

Before her marriage to Frank Lloyd Wright (opposite), Olgivanna Hinzenberg studied under Georgei Gurdjieff. She is shown at right (left foreground) spinning through one of Gurdjieff's sacred dances, ritual works inspired by whirling dervishes and intended to discipline both mind and body. Olgivanna studied with Gurdjieff in France before traveling with his dance troupe to the United States, where she first met her future husband.

ing alternative lifestyles in the woods. The seekers of spiritual awakening and self-realization, who carry forward the hopes for an enlightened millennium, have borrowed heavily from the philosophies of Steiner and Gurdjieff.

Gurdjieff's early life—and to a remarkable extent, his later public life as well—is shrouded in conflicting information. He was a master at raising fog around the details of his personal history. The people who knew Gurdjieff longest and best were the most likely to regard him as an enigma. After visiting with Gurdjieff for more than fifteen years, American novelist Jean Toomer said of his teacher, "I have never known G. I never will." Biographers who have attempted to record Gurdjieff's life before 1913, when he took up residence in Moscow, have been forced to rely heavily on their subject's own accounts—a chancy proposition, since he seemed to take delight in seeding contradictory legends.

As near as can be determined, Gurdjieff was born in the 1870s—probably 1874—to a Greek father and an Armenian mother. His childhood home, in the Caucasus Mountains between the Black and Caspian seas, was and still is an extraordinary place for the intermingling of races and languages. More than fifty dialects are spoken in Caucasia today, and in Alexandropol and Kars—the towns of Gurdjieff's boyhood—he was likely to have been in frequent contact with Russians, Turks, Greeks, Persians, Armenians, Azerbaijanis, Khevsurs, Ossets, Tartars, and Kurds.

Amid this jumble of cultures, Gurdjieff observed many peculiar things, most of which no doubt his father, Ivan, could explain perfectly well. Gurdjieff's father was a poor man, but one with a wealth of knowledge on the local folklore. Not even Ivan, however, could fully explain the soothsayers Gurdjieff met, who seemed genuinely able to predict the future. Nor could Ivan account for the séance Gurdjieff witnessed in which the boy's dead sister allegedly appeared. In one other harrowing episode, Gurdjieff came upon a terrified boy held captive by a priest of the Kurdish religious sect known as the *Yezidje.* The victim was convinced that he was trapped in a magic circle, which was actually nothing more than a line scratched on the ground. Yet when Gurdjieff tried to drag him to safety, the boy was so terrified that he collapsed in a cataleptic trance.

Early on, Gurdjieff grew impatient with his incomplete understanding of such strange phenomena. He believed that hidden knowledge was involved, and he turned to religion in hopes of discovering it. His father, meanwhile, was conspiring with a local schoolmaster to prepare Gurdjieff for a life as both a physician and a Greek Orthodox priest.

Gurdjieff's other great obsession as he approached adulthood was the stream of mechanical inventions from Europe that began to find their way to the Caucasus. Household gadgets, industrial tools, and eventually, automobiles fired his imagination, and he undertook to teach himself their workings. Later in life, he would be sharply critical of the cultural contributions of western Europe, but he never lost his love for machines.

TO KNOW—TO UNDERSTAND—TO BE

The Science
of the Harmonious Development of Man
according to the method
of
G. I. GURDJIEFF.

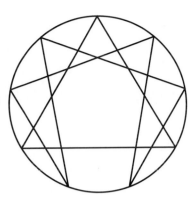

An enneagram, as Gurdjieff called this figure (ennea is Greek for nine), ornaments a symbol-laden program (left) for his Institute for the Harmonious Development of Man. The enneagram was a crucial device for Gurdjieff, who said it embodied the principles of spiritual rebirth. His followers also used the figure as a workflow diagram, believing enneagrams accurately depicted the pattern of work in real-life situations.

In his late teens or early twenties—at perhaps the same time that he finally cast aside the notion of becoming a priest—Gurdjieff hit upon a way to pursue both his great interests. He began traveling from town to town visiting monasteries, mosques, and temples and interviewed the local holy men of various religions. As he pursued his hunt for secret knowledge, he scratched out a living as a fix-it man, equipped with a traveling workshop.

For fully twenty years, Gurdjieff followed his nose to what he hoped would be the living sources of spiritual wisdom in northern Africa, eastern Europe, or central Asia. His quest at times had a slightly desperate quality: He was easily disenchanted with his teachers and quick to fly off in pursuit of the next promising lead. At one time or another, he shared the harsh existence of Christian monks, trained as a dervish, made a pilgrimage to Mecca, studied with Sufi, Hindu, and Buddhist masters, and latched onto numerous Western occult brotherhoods.

He lived by his wits. If he failed to find employment as a repairman, he traded carpets, foodstuffs, or clothing. There is reason to suspect that he sometimes engaged in petty thievery and at least once was employed as a spy.

One biographer believes that Gurdjieff may have been the principal Russian agent in Tibet during an explosive period just after the turn of the century, when the Dalai Lama was seeking the aid of imperial Russia in blocking China's and Great Britain's attempts to seize control of the mountain kingdom. Gurdjieff later wrote of his propensity during this period for placing himself in the path of revolutions and civil wars. He claimed that his sole aim was to discover some way of countering the human predilection for falling into a sort of mass hypnosis in times of social upheaval. Whether Gurdjieff's motivations were so purely altruistic is not clear, but it was certainly the case that one of his chief interests was hypnotism. At any rate, put himself at risk he did, and he apparently paid the price by sustaining serious gunshot wounds on three separate occasions.

It was while recovering from the last of these woundings—in 1904, during a time of political unrest in the Caucasus—that Gurdjieff decided to end his years of searching. Assessing the fruits of his long quest, he was thunderstruck by the sudden realization that he had within himself all the same possibilities that God had at his disposal. "The difference between Him and myself," Gurdjieff wrote, "must lie only in scale." He felt as if he had been "reincarnated," and set out to teach a more enlightened way of living.

Gurdjieff first took his message to Russia and by 1915 was attracting small clusters of disciples in St. Petersburg and Moscow. He went to great lengths to delineate the chaotic mess that had come to characterize human nature. He used the metaphor of a three-story house to sum up what he felt was a generalized abuse of human potential. On the ground floor, he taught, each individual had centers for three important bodily functions: physical movement, instinct, and sex. The second story was an emotional center, while the upper floor held the capacity for intelligence. Gurdjieff believed the world contained three types of people, each dominated by a different "floor" and neglecting the other two. The great run of humanity, he believed, had little awareness of the capacities on the second and third stories.

In Gurdjieff's view, the personality existed in two states—sleep and the ordinary waking state, which was itself a sort of slumber since it induced most people to lose sight of their essence or true value. Gurdjieff suggested that human beings must aspire to a higher state of awareness, which he referred to as self-consciousness. This was a true understanding of one's identity. Beyond self-consciousness lay an even more advanced state of awareness that Gurdjieff called objective consciousness. In this condition, human beings could hope to achieve an understanding of God.

Few people, Gurdjieff asserted, ever become aware of the need to rise above the ordinary waking state. And most of those who do recognize the need have a difficult time achieving advanced states of consciousness without the guidance of a teacher who is further along on the path of spiritual development.

Gurdjieff told his Russian disciples of the three tradi-

In the 1920s, Gurdjieff made his headquarters at Le Prieuré (above), a former residence of Madame de Maintenon, the second wife of Louis XIV. Inside a study house near the château, exotic decor (inset) reflected Eastern influences on Gurdjieff's thinking.

tional ways to follow such a path that he had observed in the religions of the world. The Hindu fakir denied his own physical needs or caused himself perpetual pain in order to develop an unbending will. But he was isolated on the first story of Gurdjieff's metaphorical house. The Christian monk was a second-story man, achieving a form of self-mastery by transcending emotional wants and needs through sheer devotion and faith. But he, too, neglected to follow the other avenues of fulfillment. The yogi achieved profound understanding by exercising his intellectual capacities, but his outlook was dry and impotent because he failed to develop his emotional powers.

Gurdjieff taught an approach he called the Work. It involved physical, emotional, and intellectual training and embodied many aspects of Eastern mysticism, carefully tailored to make them accessible to Western practitioners.

Gurdjieff's teaching in Moscow and St. Petersburg was uprooted by the turmoil of World War I and the Russian Revolution. In 1917, he fled with a small group of followers, first to Essentuki in the Caucasus, and later to Tiflis, Constantinople, and Berlin. After several years of wandering as refugees, Gurdjieff and his band finally settled in France. At a château in the forest of Fontainebleau, they established a sort of retreat house called the Institute for the Harmonious Development of Man, and Gurdjieff began to attract a loyal following of writers and intellectuals.

During Gurdjieff's time at Fontainebleau, the Work increasingly focused on encouraging students to *act* rather than to analyze. One of his favorite maxims was: "The highest that a man can attain is to be able to *do*." Ritual dance became a prominent feature of his disciples' training. In theory, the dances served to shock the "ground-floor" centers of movement and instinct out of their accustomed patterns. The training also incorporated a somewhat painful process of self-observation, which Gurdjieff spurred on by serving as a brutally frank critic of egos and personalities. Every moment of the day was treated as a time for creating self-awareness and spiritual attunement.

Gurdjieff's following in certain phases of his career—particularly the first years in France—included some influential people. Author Katherine Mansfield was one of his students, as were J. B. Priestley and American architect Frank Lloyd Wright. Unfortunately, Gurdjieff had the unsettling habit of swearing his devotees to secrecy, and in most cases they honored this pledge. Only rarely did followers proselytize their beliefs or even allow them to be known. As a result, Gurdjieff's influence at the time of his death may not have extended to more than a few hundred people.

It is all the more remarkable, therefore, that Gurdjieff's following today may number in the tens of thousands. In the mid-1930s, Gurdjieff seemed to stormily part company with most of his longtime supporters. He vanished almost entirely during World War II, and when he reappeared in the years before his death in 1949, he was bearing the fruits of ten years of assiduous writing. The master had recorded ten volumes of his thoughts and remembrances, and these have inspired new generations to carry on the Work.

His admirers today are every bit as tight-lipped as the disciples Gurdjieff swore to secrecy. More visible are the contributions of Gurdjieff's contemporary, anthroposophy originator Rudolf Steiner.

Steiner was born in 1861 in Kraljevec, Yugoslavia. Both his parents were Austrian by birth, and the father—a tele-graph operator for a railway company—moved the family back to his homeland before the son was two years old. Although the Steiners were relatively poor, Rudolf's earliest memories of the mountains and valleys of southern Austria were lyric and joyous. The happiness was short-lived, however. When Rudolf turned seven, his father accepted a job as stationmaster in the town of Neudörfl, Hungary, and the boy was thrust into a discouragingly harsh social climate. To his dismay, he found that Hungarians treated Austrians as second-class citizens.

To brace himself against this hostility, he relied more and more on his own inner resources. And from the start, he was an unusual child. By his own account, he was aware even as a toddler of an unseen world that he would later call the realm of spirit. As an adult, he described a number of unusual experiences that befell him before the age of ten.

At one point, he claimed, a vision of a woman appeared to him, woefully calling out for help. Without thinking much about it, he knew that she had recently departed the physical world. Sometime later, by his account, he would discover that a relative had committed suicide on the day he was visited by this apparition.

The airy beings that Steiner sensed at every turn sometimes seemed more real to him than the evidence of his physical perceptions. He realized, however, that most people did not share his sensitivities, and he resolved to keep his impressions to himself. Outwardly affable, he nonetheless became a lonely child, steadfastly silent on the matters that troubled him most. He buried himself in solitary recreations and thought deeply about the small details of the world around him. He was fascinated, for example, by

British author Katherine Mansfield came to Le Prieuré in 1922 already terminally ill with tuberculosis. Her death there three months later at the age of thirty-four gave rise to unfounded rumors of mistreatment that seriously hurt the institute's reputation.

A man of many interests, Rudolf Steiner (left) applied his anthroposophical insights to fields as diverse as metallurgy, beekeeping, and farming. Among several odd but apparently effective fertilizers he developed was one that was made from yarrow blossoms packed into a stag's bladder and buried for several months.

the paraphernalia of writing and took delight in such materials as the sand used to dry fresh ink on paper. It did not follow, however, that he enjoyed writing himself. In fact, he was slow to learn to read and write—an experience that made a deep impression on him and would have reverberations in his theories on education.

If words were slow to take hold, numbers were not. Later in life, Steiner recalled finding happiness for the first time in the study of geometry. Theorems on the paths of parallel lines and the angles of isosceles triangles became grist for hours of wonder and speculation. Especially pleasing to the boy was his sense that the imagined rectangles, rhomboids, and circles that he manipulated in his exercises were just as real and useful as those he discovered in the physical world. He regarded this as confirmation of his secret inner life. With vast relief he took it to heart that there was at least one area of intellectual discourse—geometry—in which the

seen and the unseen were equally meaningful realities.

Steiner attended the Technical High School in Wiener Neustadt, where his father urged him to study civil engineering. The teachers at the school were impressed by the boy's abilities and made certain that his curriculum emphasized the sciences. In his spare time, however, Rudolf took to reading philosophy. At fourteen, he bought a copy of Immanuel Kant's *Critique of Pure Reason* and waded time and again through its dense prose. He was convinced that the book held great meaning for him but was ultimately disappointed.

In the work—which is Kant's masterpiece—the author suggests that there is no way for human beings to have certainty of knowledge regarding either material phenomena or spiritual ideas. The argument struck home for many of Kant's contemporaries, but Steiner decided that it was patently incorrect. No philosophical treatise, no matter how cogently reasoned, could persuade him to turn his back on his

Four wall-hanging seals commissioned by Steiner for Anthroposophical Society meetings depict his enigmatic but hopeful visions of humanity's future. Above, a white-robed figure uses mental energy to create a sword, a feat that exhibits one of many powers Steiner believed human beings would eventually acquire. At left, a woman who has merged with the sun defeats human evil, represented by a seven-headed monster and crescent moon; in the next seal (below), an angelic figure harnesses evil to the service of good. At right, transfigured humanity appears as an ethereal cloud, encompassing the book of all knowledge and surrounded in turn by a rainbow, Steiner's emblem of the creative force.

clairvoyant perceptions. In reaction—and rebellion—he undertook a lifelong mission of scholarship.

With the optimism of youth, Steiner resolved to master all the great philosophical and scientific ideas of his day. Reading voraciously, he put himself in the minds of Nietzsche and Georg Wilhelm Friedrich Hegel. He considered the views of Karl Marx and even bumped heads with the positivism of Auguste Comte, who denied the existence of any world beyond that of the senses. Moving on to the Vienna Institute of Technology, he methodically explored Darwinism and the scientific orthodoxy of the late 1800s.

Steiner knew that if he was ever going to publicly set forth his perceptions of humanity's spiritual capabilities, he could be convincing only if he took into account the latest teachings of science and philosophy. His formal curriculum revolved around mathematics, chemistry, and physics, but he devoted as much time to foraging through modern philosophy. He devoured the writings of Fichte, Schelling, Herbart, Haeckel, and many other thinkers. Yet most of what he found was frustration. He was hoping to uncover at least one contemporary philosopher who acknowledged the spiritual world as a reality.

The first breakthrough for the young Steiner arrived unexpectedly and was unrelated to his formal schooling. On the train that he rode each week to Vienna, he happened to fall into conversation with a rough-hewn country fellow named Felix Koguski. This man earned his living gathering medicinal herbs, which he sold to apothecaries in Vienna. He spoke openly of his own acquaintance with spirits, a familiarity he claimed to have acquired through his intimacy with plants. Koguski comforted Steiner with assurances that he, too, had tried with little success to find in books

Colored Portals to the Spirit World

In most cultures, colors have a special significance. Many Westerners associate red with anger and green with life. But for Rudolf Steiner, the meaning of color went much deeper. He came to view it as a rare opening between the physical and spirit worlds.

Through his clairvoyant sense, Steiner perceived a distinct spirit meaning in each color. A shade of magenta called peach blossom was for him "the living image of the soul," visible in the astral selves of humans, animals, and plants. Green, its opposite, represented life without spirit.

The spiritual significance of color permeated Steiner's plans for everything from schoolrooms to theatrical costumes. It also led him to develop a color-based method of painting that he applied to his own works (right).

Steiner thought paintings should be constructed "out of color" rather than out of shapes. Hard lines were unnecessary. Layers of color could be used to create fluid images out of which forms and boundaries would arise.

Since much depended on getting just the right shades, Steiner proposed that artists prepare their own paints from wild plants. Such paints remain popular today for their unusual luminosity.

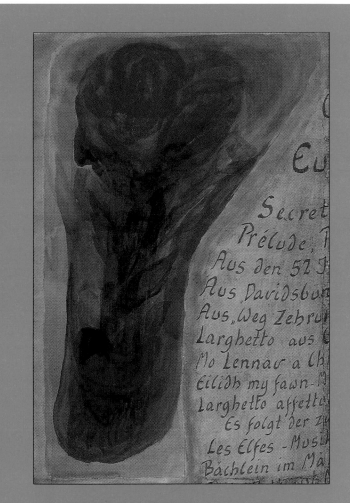

A wash of watery blue envelops the separate components of a plant in Steiner's Original Plant, found in the margin of one of his dance manuscripts.

"what he already knew for himself." The young student and the elderly woodsman struck up a lasting friendship.

Having at last found a conversational outlet for his concerns, Steiner made his next advance through his studies—he discovered the poetry of Johann Wolfgang von Goethe. In the writings of Goethe, Steiner felt certain that he had met a second kindred spirit. For one thing, Goethe shared his passion for science, having produced studies in anatomy, botany, and optics. But Goethe also seemed to have an ear for the voices of nature, and he let them speak through his poems. Steiner seized upon Goethe as a role model: a thinking and expressive man who synthesized the data of both the sciences and the soul.

While still an undergraduate, Steiner was hired by a publisher to edit a collection of Goethe's scientific writings. At about the same time, he began supplementing his income by tutoring schoolchildren, and in the course of this work he became involved with a troubled lad named Otto. Today, this youngster would probably be regarded as autistic: He was unable to relate to the world around him and seemed to be mentally retarded. After working with Otto for a short time, Steiner proposed to the parents that he be allowed to personally conduct the child's education. The parents agreed, and Steiner began improvising teaching techniques geared to Otto's very particular needs. His experiments were successful, and within two years, he was able to bring about a dramatic reversal in the boy's disabilities. Otto eventually obtained a medical degree and became a practicing physician. The lessons of this experience also exerted an influence on Steiner's theories of education. He felt that successful teaching could arise only from deep knowledge of the students on the part of the instructor.

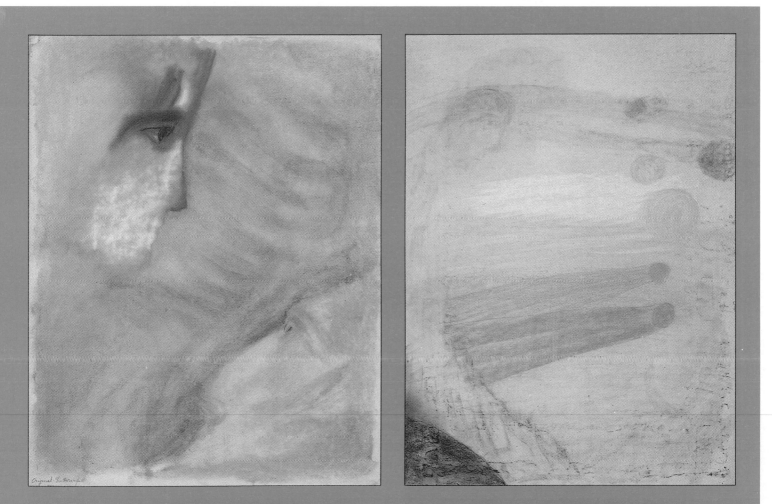

Yellow-red Lucifer, spirit of light, gazes across a green void toward Ahriman, spirit of darkness, in this 1923 Steiner pastel.

Steiner sketched Man in Relation to the Planets (above) during a two-day lecture course in which he described parallels between the human body and the cosmos.

At the age of twenty-five, Steiner published a book on Goethean philosophy, followed five years later by a doctoral thesis, which was an attack on Kant's theory of knowledge. On the strength of these works, he was offered a post at the Goethe-Schiller Archives in the German city of Weimar. There he was thrust into a rich intellectual milieu swarming with artists, writers, and academicians. He thrived during the seven years he spent in Goethe's home city, cementing a reputation as an insightful and productive scholar. Steiner lectured on a wide variety of scientific topics and published book after book on such German thinkers as Nietzsche, Arthur Schopenhauer, and Jean Paul. Steiner would remain throughout his life a prolific writer, in total publishing more than sixty books and delivering more than 6,000 lectures.

During Steiner's time in Weimar, he took his first tentative steps toward throwing off the bounds of academic convention. In his *Philosophy of Spiritual Activity,* published in 1893, he broached the idea that humankind could indeed acquire knowledge that went beyond the material world. This notion, which Steiner repeated in additional works on Nietzsche and Goethe written over the next four years, conflicted so directly with the mainstream of German philosophy that it was roundly ignored.

In 1897, Steiner became the editor of a scholarly publication called the *Review of Literature,* moving to Berlin to accept the post. The three years that followed were extremely difficult ones for him. He was plagued by financial worries and personal doubts. It bothered Steiner greatly that none of his scholarly achievements had come in the arena that mattered to him most, that he was yet unable to kindle any interest in his views on the supernatural. Greatly troubled, he plunged into a generalized study of religion that quickly found its focus in Christianity. What emerged was a highly personal view of the role of Christ in history.

Steiner was convinced that humankind had passed through an era when all people had been as clairvoyant as he and could peer into the spiritual realm. As people acquired a better understanding of the physical world, however, they had become obsessed with it and had lost their clairvoyance. Knowledge of the spirit world had all but disappeared, kept alive only through the efforts of what Steiner called the mystery centers. These were holy places scattered worldwide, where generations of initiates had studied the ancient spiritual wisdom at the feet of their elders.

According to Steiner, Christ had played an important part in this process, because he taught the spiritually aware that they must move beyond the mere preservation of their

founded the Theosophical Society to promote the study of Eastern religions and the occult. Interest in Blavatsky's work was spreading rapidly in Germany.

Steiner's unorthodox views on Christ did not mesh very neatly with the beliefs of the Theosophists. They regarded Jesus as just one of a long line of avatars—gods who had become men for the purpose of instructing the human race. Nevertheless, the organization invited Steiner to mobilize a German branch of their movement. He undertook the task and, for more than a decade, would describe his outlook as "Theosophical." In a lecture that Steiner delivered in October of 1902, he declared that his newly found purpose in life was to establish "methods of spiritual research on a scientific basis." A few years later, he would look back on this speech as the birth of anthroposophy.

His affiliation with the Theosophical Society would last eleven years and would spread Steiner's reputation beyond the narrow confines of German academia. As his star rose among the seekers and freethinkers of Theosophy, it fell just as quickly in the universities and intellectual circles where he had made his career. In that sphere there was little tolerance for discussions of mysticism or anything smacking of the paranormal. For Steiner, however, there was no turning back.

In 1909, he published *An Outline of Occult Science,* a work that sketched the elaborate cosmology and historical view that he had begun working out during his troubled first years in Berlin. The book presented the idea that humankind had chosen to hide from itself its once-direct connection to the spiritual realm. Steiner lamented that Western society had become so hardened in its denial of the spiritual connection that even individuals who struggled to reclaim their spiritual consciousnesses found it terribly difficult to do so. The challenge, Steiner suggested, was to reverse the trend and make spiritual awakening possible for all.

Steiner parted ways with the Theosophical Society in 1913, when Madame Blavatsky's successor—an English-

knowledge and actively search for perfect freedom and love. Steiner found that even in his darkest despair he had the strength to take up this search by pondering Christ's message. He began to view the coming of Christ as the central event in the cosmic evolution. The mystery of Christ's life, he believed, should enable people to recognize themselves as individuals apart from the material world.

After 1900, Steiner was a changed man. He felt increasingly free to address the topics closest to his heart. He lectured now on the fairy tales of Goethe and mystical practices of medieval Europe. He read widely on the Eastern religions and attempted to reconcile those philosophies with the wisdom of the Christian gospels. Somewhat to his own surprise, he found a ready-made audience for his wide-ranging lecture topics. In large measure, the new receptiveness was due to the influence of Helena Blavatsky, a flamboyant Russian medium and mystic. Madame Blavatsky had

Antonio Gaudi (right) devised the playful lizard water fountain below as part of his design for Guell Park in Barcelona. Named for Gaudi's patron Eusebio Guell, this residential development involved houses built on triangular tracts of land on Mount Pelada, with views of the city and ocean. Guell Park's dominant motif was its colorful mosaic tile, which decorated plazas, stairways, sidewalks, and two highly ornamented administration buildings.

Natural Impulses of an Architectural Genius

Nature, according to Spanish architect Antonio Gaudi, is God's architecture. Man-made structures, he said, should imitate natural forms. That logic led Gaudi to develop an undulating, organic style of building that brought the look of a rural utopia to urban streets.

It was a welcome innovation for turn-of-the-century Barcelona, reeling under rapid industrial growth. Gaudi's rippling walls and curving roofs humanized new neighborhoods and revitalized old ones. His projects ranged from apartment complexes and bridges to the smaller structures shown below. One commission dominated his last forty-two years: the Church of the Sagrada Familia, or Holy Family.

Seen partially completed at right, the soaring Sagrada Familia was intended to rank among Europe's great cathedrals. Gaudi poured his naturalistic, quasi-mystical impulses into it. Struts and towers blended seamlessly, as if grown from the same seed; sculpted turtles and snails replaced conventional gargoyles; turrets resembled trees.

As he built the church, Gaudi became increasingly devout, eventually choosing to live in poverty. This decision may have hastened his death. Struck by a streetcar in 1926, the poorly clad architect was mistaken for a vagrant and received minimal care for several hours before he was recognized. He died three days later.

His unique architectural legacy was ignored outside Barcelona until the 1960s. Today his work is ranked among the earliest and most successful attempts to restore human scale to the modern city.

Not one straight line can be found in the naturalistic masonry of this entrance gate, designed by Gaudi in 1902 for a private Barcelona home.

woman named Annie Besant—decreed that Christ had reincarnated as the Indian guru Jiddu Krishnamurti. Steiner withdrew from Besant's organization immediately and announced the formation of his own group, the Anthroposophical Society. Many German Theosophists followed suit, and from that day forward Steiner enjoyed the emotional and financial support of a growing band of disciples.

Ever the prolific writer, he began to assert his influence in other areas as well. He renewed an interest in painting and sculpture, convinced that he could help to move those arts forward to a freer and more expressive future. Like Gurdjieff, he developed his own form of spiritually attuned dance, called eurhythmy. This was a system of flowing movements performed to the rhythms of spoken language and music. Beginning in 1910, Steiner introduced a series of dramatic interpretations of his cosmological teachings.

These dramas, which he called mystery plays, brought to life his ideas on reincarnation and human interaction with spirit beings. As the stage presentations became more elaborate, Steiner saw the value in acquiring a theater that would be architecturally appropriate to the mood and message of his dramas. Finding no facility that provided such a setting, he took it upon himself to design a building that he called the Goetheanum. The structure, which was completed in 1920 at the village of Dornach near Basel, Switzerland, was marked by the unusual architectural feature of twin domes giving shape to a single room. An enormous cupola spanned the great hall of the theater with a smaller dome below to set off the stage area. Steiner took up residence in Dornach, and other members of the Anthroposophical Society expressed an interest in building homes adjacent to the Goetheanum.

Steiner had no wish to be the head of a sect. His vision of the movement he had founded was global in scope, and he believed that the values he was espousing could be em-braced wherever his followers might live. For a time, therefore, he resisted the idea of establishing a permanent community at Dornach. But he eventually gave in to the wishes of his colleagues and came to think of the place as a seed for the flowering of worldwide anthroposophy.

In the years immediately following World War I, Steiner directed the spread of the anthroposophical movement to many different parts of the world. During this time he also turned his attention to two projects—agriculture and education—that would eventually yield some of his most visible and lasting contributions.

On the agricultural front, Steiner believed that the soil of a garden or farm was a living organism with its own spiritual nature. Moving from this premise, he argued that modern intensive-farming techniques were depleting the soil by robbing it of its spirit, and he proposed a solution called biodynamic farming. Many of the practices that Steiner suggested—extensive crop rotation, the sowing of certain plants that raise the nitrogen level of the soil, and the heavy use of compost—are today standard practice for organic farmers.

The educational principles that Steiner championed grew out of his conviction that cultivation of the mind was just one aspect of a school's responsibilities. Spiritual and emotional development he considered every bit as important. A striking feature of Steiner's philosophy was that chil-

that a student could be considered ready for the pursuit of spiritual clairvoyance. Anthroposophy, therefore, was never a part of the Steiner curriculum. The quest for spiritual advancement, he insisted, could be fruitful only if it was freely entered into by mature adults.

Steiner's ideas on education were initially put in practice at the request of a group of Stuttgart industrialists seeking better schools for the children of their employees. The first institution was formed at a tobacco factory called Waldorf Astoria, and the Waldorf, or Steiner, schools—as they came to be called—have proliferated ever since, particularly in Europe and North America. Today there are nearly 500 schools worldwide that operate on the principles Steiner set out.

dren should not be taught to read until the age of seven or eight, when their adult teeth grew in. He believed that this physical event signaled an important spiritual transition. At earlier stages, Steiner suggested, children could learn only by imitating their environment. Early childhood, therefore, was best reserved for the formation of loving relationships. Beyond this stage, children became capable of imaginative knowledge, and for the next seven years they could benefit from instruction in such areas as science, history, art, and music. These were taught not as unrelated subjects but as different dimensions of a single human endeavor.

With the onset of puberty, the capacity for inspiration fell within a child's grasp, and the arts and sciences could finally be presented as specialized undertakings. In Steiner's view, it was not until age twenty-one, or thereabout,

While Steiner was acutely aware of the reality of evil in the world, his overall view was one of evolutionary optimism. He believed that it was the destiny of humanity to rise to a higher state of consciousness. In the meantime, he felt, people of all kinds could take positive steps to open themselves up to their spiritual nature. On these matters he differed from Gurdjieff, who believed that the vast majority of people were too set in their ways to change their mode of learning about themselves and addressing the world around them. But both men reached the same conclusions about the narrow path to utopia: It could be reached solely through the process of perfecting the human spirit.

The solitary mission of the visionary artist found vivid expression in Wenzel Hablik's 1918 painting, The Path of Genius. As a lone climber (upper right), arms outstretched in triumph, approaches his mountaintop reward, less persistent seekers lie beaten or trapped on cliffs and outcrops below. The possibility of being misunderstood or ridiculed, Hablik felt, should not deter true believers from the quest. "Artists who do not create with a feeling for the cosmic and universal," he wrote, "have nothing to do with real creation."

An Obligation "to Redo Everything"

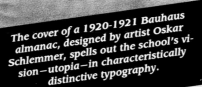

The cover of a 1920-1921 Bauhaus almanac, designed by artist Oskar Schlemmer, spells out the school's vision—utopia—in characteristically distinctive typography.

Between 1910 and 1930, Europe was ravaged by war and racked by economic turmoil. For many artists and intellectuals, each new shock only added greater urgency to their pleas for a complete break with the past. Since before the turn of the century, the European intelligentsia had grown increasingly fixated on the idea that the existing social institutions needed to be reexamined and challenged. "The artist's obligation," concluded the Russian writer Alexander Blok, "is to redo everything."

Many members of Europe's avant-garde were veterans of World War I. Appalled by the slaughter and destruction they had witnessed, they created new art forms that they hoped might counter the madness that had caused the conflagration. Some artists linked their hopes for change to the revolutionary political movements that swept aside the prewar regimes of Germany and Russia. Others sought refuge in the consciousness-raising techniques of Eastern religions, incorporating yoga and meditation into the practice of their arts.

In language as unbounded as their aspirations, they called themselves futurists, suprematists, constructivists, and expressionists. They congregated in formal schools such as the Bauhaus of Weimar, Germany, in loosely organized movements such as de Stijl of the Netherlands, and in secretive alliances such as the Crystal Chain. At international exhibitions and art shows, they shared their idiosyncratic visions for a utopian future. And they carried their ideas to a wider audience with printed propaganda and theatrical publicity stunts.

Despite differences in language, culture, and religion, the avant-garde of this period shared a fundamental idealism. They rejected elitist notions such as "art for art's sake," preferring more egalitarian work that would be accessible to the masses. In technique, they were deliberately provocative, hoping, by its shock value, to draw viewers into their art and stimulate strong reactions.

Though bound by a common sense of urgency regarding the need for change, they did not necessarily agree on the details of their objectives. For some, like Russian painter Wassily Kandinsky, utopia was a purely spiritual state that was approachable only through concentrated mental effort. Many others awaited an earthly paradise and believed that their art could prepare the way.

In the past, science and technology had often been decried by utopians. Now, they were embraced as a hopeful fact of modern life. The futurists found beauty in smoke-belching factories and backfiring automobiles. They reasoned that if labor-saving machinery and mass production could make the necessities of life more accessible, humankind would be freed to pursue loftier objectives.

Avant-garde painters adopted abstract styles as the most suitable mode for expressing transcendental themes. Some, in their zeal for communication, reduced their artistic vocabulary to the most basic geometric shapes.

Artists in other fields, including music, drama, dance, and design, were also caught up in the movement for change. Architects were among the most daring proponents of the new sensibilities. Forsaking stone and wood, they rushed to make use of steel, glass, and reinforced concrete. Their fanciful designs for cities of sky-loving towers and interwoven freeways rarely moved beyond the blueprint stage. But they triumphed in capturing the cosmic spirit of the day.

"The Radiant Splendor of Our Future"

In the view of poet Filippo Marinetti, Italy had lived too long in the past, absorbed in its Roman and Renaissance glories. With a cadre of like-minded artists, he launched the futurist movement in 1909 with an inflammatory call for the destruction of the nation's art academies, libraries, and museums.

Casting aside conventional themes, the futurists sought fresh inspiration in the dazzling potential of modern technology and the vitality of industrial cities. Their enthusiasm for the age of the machine was infectious and uninhibited. "Nothing is more beautiful," an ebullient Marinetti gushed, "than a great humming central electric station."

Not surprisingly, the products of modern engineering, from speeding cars to suspension bridges, were often the subjects of futurist art. But the futurists also put new technology to use in their efforts to blaze new artistic frontiers. One musician created an orchestra of amplified noisemakers to glorify the din of industrial plants; other artists turned to photography in hopes of better capturing the dynamism of modern life.

Issuing manifestoes in half a dozen languages, the futurists described themselves as "free moderns, who are confident in the radiant splendor of our future." Trumpeting the call for a break with the past in public events that sometimes ended in riots, Marinetti promoted his cause with such energy that the press dubbed him the Caffeine of Europe. Behind the deliberate provocations, however, lay a serious purpose. Technology, Marinetti believed, could produce a society of great abundance, and futurist art would hasten the arrival of that utopia by creating new ways of seeing, hearing, and thinking.

The futurist obsessions with speed and force are evident in Dynamism of an Automobile, *a 1913 work by Luigi Russolo. While the racing car is visible only in its blurred contours, sharply defined wedges and lines capture the sensation of velocity by suggesting speed-induced shock and sound waves.*

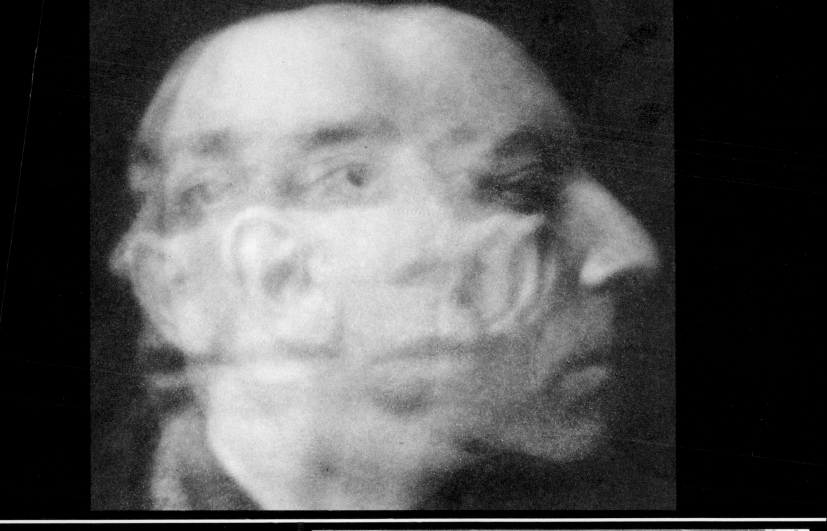

Photodynamism of Boccioni
was created around 1915 by
photographer Giannetto Bisi.
The ghostly multiple exposures
of painter Umberto Boccioni
illustrate two signature traits of
futurist art: emphasis on a
subject's inner essence rather
than its external appearance
and the attempt to convey the
sensation of movement.

Luigi Russolo and an assistant
demonstrate the operation of
Noise Intoners, special-purpose
speakers that produced the
sounds of explosions, rattles,
squeaks, and buzzes so as to
simulate the hubbub of a modern factory. A painter turned
musician, Russolo considered
his lack of musical training an
asset, since he hoped to remake
the entire concept of music.

In his search for spiritual enlightenment, Russian suprematist painter Kazimir Malevich (right) abandoned the classical themes of art and restricted his work to the most basic shapes and colors. Malevich hoped that his stark 1918 oil painting, White on White (below), would make viewers feel they were floating free of any bounds.

"Rising Above the Laws of Necessity"

Between 1914 and 1920, the Russian art world was shaken by a revolt that paralleled the political upheaval of the 1917 Bolshevik Revolution. Two radical artistic philosophies, suprematism and constructivism, competed for the allegiance of Russian artists. The movements were related in their pioneering use of abstract styles, but they had distinct goals and offered contrasting visions of utopia.

The father of suprematism, poet and painter Kazimir Malevich, regarded all art as a potentially powerful inspirational tool, but he disavowed the representational styles of the past. "Only the abstract elevates [man] to a truly higher spiritual level," he wrote. "Only by developing new forms, by rising above the laws of necessity by which objects are governed, do we see man completely liberated." Malevich and his comrades strove to distill the material world to its abstract essence and thereby lead the art-loving Russian public to address the deepest metaphysical questions.

The constructivists, by contrast, saw themselves not as spiritual guides but as creative engineers. Like Marinetti's futurists in Italy, they welcomed advances in science and technology and applied their skills to the real-world problems of architecture and industrial design. Despite this practical orientation, the constructivists were deeply idealistic. They believed that art should play a critical role in rebuilding the shattered Russian society.

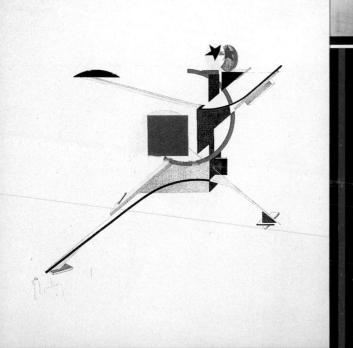

In a 1924 photomontage, Con-
structor: Self-Portrait (above),
Muscovite painter El Lissitzky
adapted the abstract style of his
suprematist teachers to the
more down-to-earth goals of
the constructivist movement.
Here, Lissitzky evokes the mer-
its of precision and practical
utility by superimposing images
of his face and his hand holding
an architect's compass onto a
background of graph paper.
The geometrical components of
The New Man (left) echo the
influences of Malevich, but the
lithograph's machinelike subject matter betrays a constructivist's preference for concrete
accomplishments over spiritual
visions. For Lissitzky, politics
was part of art: The red square
in the painting symbolizes com-
munism's social philosophy.

A tangible expression of designer Bruno Taut's architectural dreams, the Glass Pavilion (below) dazzled visitors to the 1914 German Werkbund Exhibition in Cologne. The structure's double-glazed, colored-glass dome sheltered a chamber that was surrounded by ornate glass walls. The interior, bathed in a soft kaleidoscope of light, featured a multilevel waterfall whose sounds contributed to the serenity. Taut had little patience for the persistent questioning by visitors regarding the building's purpose. "The Glashaus has no other function," he snapped, "than to be beautiful."

"Imaginary Architects"

German architect Bruno Taut found silver linings in the darkest clouds. In 1919, with the construction industry in a slump, Taut turned financial deficiency into creative opportunity. "Let us consciously be imaginary architects," he urged a dozen colleagues, and then began a secretive correspondence group, the Crystal Chain, to design soaring fantasies of glass.

One of the group's guiding spirits was Paul Scheerbart, a deceased author whose mystical novels introduced Taut to the supposed powers of crystal. "A person who daily sets eyes on the splendors of glass," Scheerbart had written, "cannot do wicked deeds." Taut combined his favorite author's faith in crystal with his own belief that architecture—the most people-oriented form of art—could lead the way to social and moral renewal.

Members of the Crystal Chain delighted in the conspiratorial nature of their cabal, exchanging ideas and blueprints under pseudonyms and publishing sketches in esoteric journals. Secrecy also shielded members from criticism by their more conventional colleagues. Glass design, gibed the brick-and-mortar architects, was thoroughly impractical—better suited to jewelry boxes or Tiffany lampshades.

If the Crystal Chain's visions stood little chance of realization, Taut felt certain that the fault was not in the fantasy. The practical obstacles to building crystal utopias would vanish, he believed, as soon as architects created a suitable aesthetic consciousness.

With designs that evoked the splendors of medieval cathedrals and monasteries, Wenzel Hablik and Max Taut exhibited the Crystal Chain's predilection for symbols of purity and innocence. In Max Taut's ornate Blossom House design (left), floral-shaped roof trusses were depicted bursting into crystalline bloom, while the sparkling glass facets of Hablik's Crystal House (below) would complement a pristine mountaintop setting. Hablik and his colleagues envisioned their structures as temples of a new, secular religion—one that would have no clergy. Hablik believed that the beauty of glass would make clear to all beholders "the divine strength of their own hearts."

The Cathedral of the Future, a woodcut by Lyonel Feininger, graced the cover of the Bauhaus manifesto. The communal efforts of artists, architects, and craftsmen were represented by the trinity of stars whose beams intersected over the cathedral's Gothic spires. The cathedral symbolized the spirit of artistic interaction and teamwork that the Bauhaus artists hoped to nurture at their academy. "The new structure of the future," declared the manifesto, would "one day rise toward heaven from the hands of a million workers."

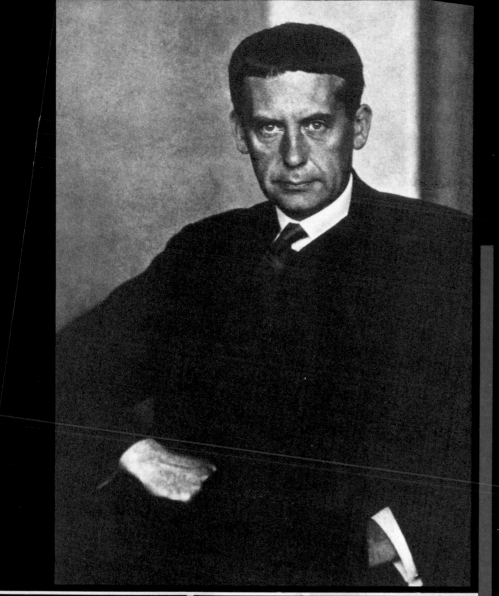

As director of the Bauhaus, Walter Gropius (above) brought flair to his mission of integrating art with life. In addition to presiding over a faculty of brilliant but temperamental artists, he fought off right-wing charges of political subversion and left-wing accusations that Bauhaus art had no functional value. In his own office (right), Gropius displayed the harmonious integration of form and function that came to characterize Bauhaus design.

Seeking "the Total Work of Art"

Walter Gropius had revolution in mind when he founded his school of design, the Bauhaus, in 1919. A gifted architect, he had come to believe that it was a mistake to make the education of architects and industrial designers any different from that of painters, sculptors, and graphic artists. At the Bauhaus he abolished all such distinctions. But this educational radicalism was only a small part of his larger, visionary agenda.

Gropius was one of those who had recently returned from the killing fields of World War I. He believed—along with many others of his time—that art must transform the moral and ethical climate that had allowed humankind to degenerate. The name Gropius chose for his academy evoked the tradition of the *Bauhütten*—medieval guilds of building tradesmen that had once thrived in Germany. His aim was not to step back into the past but to reestablish a lost sense of common identity and cooperation between artists and craftsmen. In a manifesto published in 1919, Gropius called upon all artists, manufacturers, builders, and craftsmen to bring about a new society in which the creative professions would merge to create "the total work of art."

Oddly enough, the builders of the future found relatively few architecture courses at the Bauhaus. With the exception of Gropius, most of the influential faculty members were painters such as Paul Klee, Johannes Itten, and Wassily Kandinsky *(overleaf)*, who were associated with the expressionist movement. Gropius believed that talented painters could open the eyes of his students to elements of form, color, and design that were common to all the arts. Students trained to see the world in new ways, he felt, would also find ways to build a better one.

As unconventional in his approach to teaching as he was in his art, Johannes Itten brought a mix of rigorous academic discipline and deeply felt mysticism to his three-year tenure as a Bauhaus instructor. His classroom methods, derived in part from his studies of an ascetic Eastern cult called Mazdaznan, included fasting, meditation, and impromptu skits in which students were called on to act out the shapes, sounds, and emotions associated with their art. In Ascent and Pause (below), which was painted in 1919, Itten demonstrated his concern for vitality as well as movement on the canvas with his trademark techniques of vivid color contrasts and energetic geometric forms.

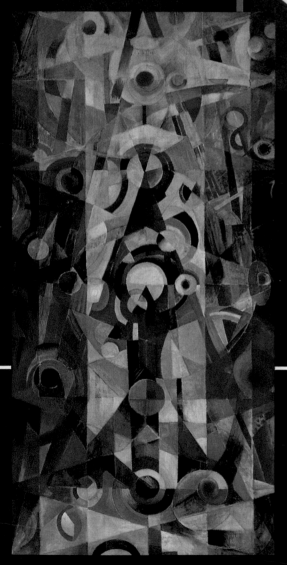

Trained as a violinist, Bauhaus instructor Paul Klee (left) compared painting to a Mozart sonata, in which numerous independent melodies blend in a harmonious whole. Klee's 1921 watercolor Dream City reflected his belief that art should be a process in which the painter adds and subtracts colors and forms until the work achieves an inner harmony. Moreover, he wanted to devise a visual language and use it to describe his view of the world. Though conventional in his teaching, Klee regarded technical excellence in painting as a means to metaphysical ends. He believed that art could penetrate "dimensions far removed from conscious endeavor."

Painter and dramatist Oskar Schlemmer (below), director of the Bauhaus Theater, used the stage to present a portrait of the utopian future, combining a metaphysical sensibility with an enthusiasm for modern technology. In productions such as the 1927 Stages of Dramatic Gesture (left), he employed mechanized sets and lighting to enhance precisely orchestrated rituals of dance and gymnastics. But Schlemmer's dancers did not reflect a mechanistic view of human value. They represented an ideal of graceful movement—a capacity that Schlemmer believed had been lost to humanity since its fall from heavenly grace.

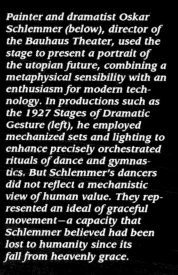

An intense spirituality infused the life and work of Russian-born Wassily Kandinsky (above), who taught at the Bauhaus from 1922 to 1933. Influenced by the suprematist theories of his countryman Kazimir Malevich, Kandinsky adopted crisp geometric shapes as an artistic language capable of transcending the emptiness of materialistic values and guiding viewers to a higher consciousness. In his 1924 oil painting, Accords Opposés (right), Kandinsky suggested such a cosmic dimension with a balanced composition in which angular, antenna-laden structures seem poised to communicate with circular, planetlike counterparts.

In Pursuit of "The Style"

Dutch painter Theo van Doesburg saw reflections of universal harmony in every aspect of life and experience. To encourage the expression of this equilibrium, he established in 1917 a journal that he called *De Stijl*—Dutch for "the style." In launching the magazine, he also gave birth to an artistic movement of the same name, which he would champion for many years to come. Van Doesburg was convinced that the perception of order, even on a small scale, would lead observers of art, architecture, and industrial design to appreciate—and to emulate in their own lives—the larger spiritual harmony of the cosmos.

Like-minded artists, designers, and craftsmen were able to assist van Doesburg in developing a consistent aesthetic approach that gave expression to this trust in an underlying harmony. Chief among the formulators of "the style" was Paris-based painter Piet Mondrian.

At the time, Mondrian was strongly influenced by the occult theories of the French Theosophists, who interpreted all human experience in terms of a balance of opposing forces. He found an abstract representation of this notion in the simple form of a right angle: There, opposing vertical and horizontal lines were united in perfect balance. With Mondrian's encouragement, rectangles—conjunctions of right-angle pairs—became a recurring motif of de Stijl art.

Also under Mondrian's sway, the de Stijl movement adopted an imperative for stylistic consistency in color. Mondrian permitted only three primary colors—yellow, blue, and red—along with three noncolor counterparts, white, black, and gray. The limited palette served to reinforce the geometric equilibrium that became a trademark of de Stijl design.

In keeping with the de Stijl ideal of harmony, Piet Mondrian designed his Paris studio (above) to reflect and reinforce the composition of his paintings. The work currently in progress in the studio blends into the geometric abstraction of the wall to its rear.

Vivid accents of primary colors and finely balanced architectural elements distinguish this two-story house in Utrecht, which was built by the Dutch artisan Gerrit Rietveld. Followers of de Stijl considered the structure to be a triumph of three-dimensional harmony.

Gerrit Rietveld's red and blue chair (left) integrates a tilted rectangular seat and backrest into a rectangular frame so precisely proportioned that no single member predominates. This 1917 design was such a perfect expression of de Stijl that Rietveld, a carpenter with no formal training in art, was invited to join the movement.

Theo van Doesburg's Counter-composition V (above) adheres to the doctrine of primary colors and rectangular forms. But van Doesburg (left) said his use of diagonals added dynamism to Mondrian's formula. Mondrian, who insisted his style was already dynamic, was so upset he left the movement.

CHAPTER 4

Toward a Planetary Vision

The German soldier was a kid about 16, his hair strung out in the bushes, still alive. The .30-caliber bullets had scooped out his chest and I saw his heart. He was gray with shock, going fast. He stared up at me—a mournful, little boy's face. He asked: 'Why did you shoot? I wanted to surrender.' "

Leo Litwak was a U.S. Army medic on that spring day in 1945, as the war in Europe neared its end. His outfit had taken a German village without resistance, and Litwak was contemplating the happy prospect of helping himself from cellars filled with sausages and wine when he heard rifle shots, followed by shouts of "Aid man!" Running over to some bushes, Litwak found the young German, mortally wounded by GIs who said he had failed to answer their demand for surrender.

Litwak shrugged off the death. That was war; war was hell. And for twenty-two years, the grim scene lay submerged, seemingly forgotten, in his subconscious mind. Yet during those years, he was nagged by a spiritual emptiness, an inexplicable numbness, as he called it. Then, in 1967, while employed as an associate professor of English at San Francisco State College, Litwak was commissioned by the *New York Times Magazine* to write an article about California's Esalen Institute, which was achieving a certain fame among groups exploring the outer edges of human potential.

To research his subject, Litwak enrolled in a five-day workshop, which at first failed to engage him. "A fat lady in leotards directed us to be absurd," he wrote. "We touched our noses with our tongues. We jumped. We ran. We clutched one another, made faces at one another."

But after his initial disdain, Litwak became engrossed as he moved through exercises in sensory awareness, fantasy experiments, and psycho-drama—in which participants act out the details of their most deeply hidden secrets. For Litwak, the cathartic climax came when he was instructed to lie down, close his eyes, and imagine that he was a "tiny self entering my own body." In the course of that trip, he suddenly saw "a heart sheathed in slime, hung with blood vessels." With a start he recognized it as the heart of the slain German soldier.

At that moment, Litwak felt a freedom, a pure and shining joy he had never experienced before. "I wailed for that German boy who had never mattered to me," he recalled, "and I heaved up my numbness. I started to feel again and discovered what I'd missed. I felt wide open, lightened, ready to meet others simply and directly."

Leo Litwak is one of thousands who testify to psychological enrichment at Esalen, where even the scenery lends enchantment. In the rugged Big Sur country, where wild boars and mountain lions still roam, Esalen's more than 100 acres nest on a cliff nearly 100 feet above the pounding waters of the Pacific. Rustic cabins nestle beside a redwood lodge, hot sulfur springs gush from the mountainside, a bountiful garden grows atop a 3,000-year-old compost heap created by the now-extinct Esalen Indians, and a cylindrical community tent, designed along traditional Mongolian lines, is called the Big Yurt.

To the wildness of Big Sur in 1962 came Michael Murphy and Richard Price, both thirty years old, both from well-to-do families, and both (although they had not known each other at the time) former psychology majors at Stanford. There Murphy had developed an interest in Eastern philosophy; after graduation and a stint in the army, he took himself to India, to a religious community called the Sri Aurobindo Ashram, where he meditated for eight hours a day. A year and a half later, Murphy returned to the United States, worked two days a week at such jobs as bellhopping, and contin- ued his contemplations. His path eventually led him to San Francisco's eccentric North Beach district, to which Richard Price had also gravitated—after serving in the air force and doing graduate work at Harvard. The two became friends, and between them, the idea of the Esalen Institute gradually emerged. "We didn't have a blue-print," Murphy later recalled. "The whole idea was exploration into consciousness in general—and the notion to support a diversity of approaches."

Murphy's grandmother was persuaded to proffer a long-term lease on property she owned in Big Sur. And almost overnight, Esalen became a 1960s bazaar for the eclectic, the esoteric, and the experimental. It offered forums, seminars, and workshops on Gestalt awareness training, somatic disciplines, psychotherapy, the meld of Eastern philosophy and Western science, mysticism, and shamanism. In so-called encounter groups, men wrestled one another to work out their hostilities, and all sorts of people stripped to expunge their inhibitions. In Esalen's soothing hot-spring baths, mixed groups of nude men and women contemplated the cosmos.

It was a heady time. "We thought we were astronauts of inner space," Murphy said later, "about to break through into new realms of consciousness. We wanted to put man on the psychic moon."

Inevitably, Esalen became a target for critics who saw it as a tower of psychobabble and a

gymnasium for group gropings. But Esalen survived and has changed with the times. Richard Price was killed in 1985 by a falling boulder, and Michael Murphy long ago gave up day-to-day direction of the institute. He does, however, remain its chairman, and he has helped steer his brainchild toward what has been called new-wave citizen diplomacy.

As a concrete and political counterpart to its marrying of Eastern and Western philosophies, Esalen in 1980 initiated a Soviet-American exchange program designed to open communication between individuals and organizations of the two superpowers. Esalen arranged a face-to-face meeting of Soviet cosmonauts and U.S. astronauts; it set up a live, two-way television link between American and Soviet rock groups; it helped organize the 1989 visit to the United States of political maverick Boris Yeltsin; and it is under Esalen auspices that a $25,000 reward has been offered to anyone who can think of a way to make a respectable international currency out of the ruble. With Mikhail Gorbachev's policies of greater openness came greater numbers of Soviets visiting the California coast and, in 1990, Esalen's first Soviet staff member.

To be sure, Esalen still practices many of its earlier techniques, but they no longer seem so mind-boggling, and of the 10,000 or so guests who annually sip the institute's "rejuvelac" cold wheat-grass juice or soak in the spas, scores are likely to be visiting officials or poets from the Soviet Union.

Esalen also has had profound effects right at home. For many of the seekers who came to partake of the institute's programs for developing human potential, the lonely perfection of the person simply was not enough. They wanted to find ways to help not just individuals but groups fulfill their best possibilities. They wanted community.

Some of Esalen's visitors have been, or have become, residents of intentional communities—cooperative groups whose members come together not by coincidence but rather in deliberate communal striving toward utopian goals. Since its inception, Esalen Institute has been regarded as a philosophical base and a skills workshop for many of the thousands of intentional communities that exist throughout the world. Through people it has trained in interpersonal communications skills, Esalen has helped communities learn to resolve conflicts and stay together.

Esalen's original form was that of an institute, where teachers and guests were transient visitors, and the organization's leaders still see it as just that. But according to some authorities on utopian communities, including Robert S. Fogarty, a history professor at Antioch College, Esalen, too, has evolved into something of an intentional community, with its own tailor-made self-governing structure and a preschool for the residents' young children.

Over the centuries, many different aspirations—economic, scholarly, spiritual—have moved people to live in intentional communities. In the United States in the 1950s, some communes were formed to practice the newly discovered spiritual disciplines of Zen Buddhism. As time went on, the failure of the government to eradicate poverty, the frustrations of the civil-rights movement, and gross abuse of the environment moved many communards to try constructing an "alternative society." Many sought to withdraw from the assassinations of John and Robert Kennedy and Martin Luther King, Jr., from the Cold War, from the Vietnam War—and, not least, from the threat of thermonuclear extinction. Many were looking for religious sanctuary. Some simply doubted the healthfulness of modern urban life.

Antioch's Professor Fogarty, along with many other authorities, dismisses the widespread notion that intentional communities proliferate in times of social ferment and die out in calmer days. He suspects that their number re-

Nude Esalen residents, fresh from hot-spring baths, curl in yoga poses before the sun as it sinks into the Pacific. Esalen's idyllic setting, among the redwoods and cypresses along California's craggy, misty coast (inset), serves as inspiration for the institute's utopian vision, which blends the old Eastern tradition of contemplation with modern California notions such as "body awareness" in the quest for self-fulfillment.

mains fairly constant but that the communities receive more attention in periods of turmoil, such as the 1960s. Recent surveys have counted from 3,000 to 10,000 intentional communities in North America alone—and every continent has its own complement. Some—like Esalen—have turned their efforts toward a sort of citizens' diplomacy. Some look to technology to eliminate drudgery and provide an environment where people can live full lives; others seek enlightenment through Eastern mysticism; many find spiritual fulfillment in charitable deeds, while many more draw strength from the soil on which they live and farm. Yet despite the diverse and idiosyncratic nature of their lifestyles and their goals, most of the people who dwell in intentional communities share the faith that they are children of what has become known as the New Age.

The so-called New Age is said to more or less coincide with the astrologi-

cal Age of Aquarius—during which the sun at the spring equinox appears in the constellation of Aquarius the Water Bearer. This period, say some students of the zodiac, began in the 1960s, will last for 2,100 years, and is characterized by a quest for harmony, peace, and understanding. The New Age, in short, is seen as a utopian era.

The New Age's philosophical Moses was the famed French paleontologist, mystic, and Jesuit priest, Pierre Teilhard de Chardin. Teilhard served as a World War I stretcher-bearer, and in the midst of death he pondered the puzzles of life and the potential of the human spirit. He became convinced that evolution was as much a spiritual as a biological process and that spiritual unity was its goal. Teilhard came to feel that humankind shared a "oneness, or *Unicity,*" that made every person part of the earth's "living envelope," or biosphere, "the living membrane which is stretched like a film over the surface of the lustrous star which holds us."

And over "this sentient protoplasmic layer," Teilhard became aware of "an ultimate envelope, taking on its own individuality and gradually detaching itself like a luminous *aura.*" This he named the *noosphere,* from the Greek *noos,* meaning "mind." This "ultimate envelope," he said, "was not only conscious but thinking, and it was always there that I found concentrated, in an ever more dazzling and consistent form, the essence or rather the very Soul of the Earth."

To Teilhard, the noosphere was the integrated mass of all consciousness, flowing together from individual humans. And in one form or another, this concept of synergized thought lies at the base of New Age philosophy.

Teilhard's writings, however, remained unpublished until after his death in 1955. By then, other profound intellects had approached the same subject from different directions. Gazing back into antiquity, historian Arnold Toynbee, who was an early visitor to Esalen,

concluded that civilizations decline not so much because of invasions or other external forces as because of an internal hardening of intellectual arteries. The "elite creative minority," he said, gives life to a civilization but is gradually replaced by another minority, dominant yet not creative.

In their interpretation of Toynbee's thesis, the inhabitants of New Age communities believe that they are the people who can best provide creative solutions to the problems confronting humankind, and that they can best shape a new stage of civilization, based on spiritual transformation and advancement in the human condition.

While Toynbee was considering the "ideo-sclerosis" of civilizations, British writer Aldous Huxley was in California making a clinical examination of Eastern mysticism. Though a skep-

Body limp and eyes closed, a woman attending an Esalen workshop entrusts herself totally to the raised hands of fellow participants, learning to relinquish control. Such exercises, designed to foster openness among participants, are seen by some as a microcosm of what New Age utopians want to do globally — knock down the barriers of misunderstanding that divide the world.

Citizens of Damanhur trained in their founder's magic try to exorcise a poltergeist from a home. Community members have been called to all parts of Italy to provide this service, for which they collect travel expenses but no fees.

Damanhurians hold hands in a spiral shape (right), hoping to open up an energy channel and awaken the god Pan. The lines on the field—two triangles forming a six-pointed star within a circle—figure in Damanhur's equinox and solstice rites.

Damanhur's reigning empress, Jaguar (below), prepares to crown a new king of one of the Game of Life teams. Called Albatross, he would lead a team named Barracuda. When this picture was taken, all teams had animal names; later they decided to adopt vegetable names.

A Paranormal Plan for the Future

Centered in the Italian countryside near Turin is Damanhur, an aspiring utopia dedicated to sound ecology, spiritual exploration, and the paranormal. Calling itself "a prototype of the future Aquarian society," Damanhur aims to "try out various living systems and publish the results." As one experiment, residents marry for a maximum three-year term—renewable if both parties agree. Of the community's 250 "citizens," one-third live on about eighty acres in the settlement near Turin, the rest in fourteen other centers around Italy they call embassies.

Although it honors Italian law, Damanhur has its own elected governors and judges and its own bank. It even has its own currency, which is accepted in several neighboring towns. Because they believe the ideal life should be playful, residents compete in a contest called the Game of Life, involving a mix of some conventional athletic events with elaborate taglike games and some purposely childish ones.

Damanhur was founded in 1975 by students of Oberto Airaudi, a parapsychologist and faith healer. Damanhurians study esoteric arts, including pre-cognition, remembering of past lives, and communication with plants. Many study Airaudi's brand of magic, based on what he calls a self. An invented name unrelated to the English word, a self is a spiral-shaped metal device, which adepts say can catch loose cosmic energies, neutralize the negative ones, and amplify the positive.

The sale of selfs is one community business; others include publishing, farming, weaving and tailoring, and the production and sale of chemical-free foods to buyers as far afield as the United States. Damanhurians also maintain a "natural-medicine" clinic, open daily, and a Sunday-afternoon esoteric and ecological market; both draw people from nearby towns.

tic and a pessimist, Huxley became convinced long before Esalen was founded that the mystical experience, the direct union of an individual with the Godhead, can be experimentally verified—and that it holds the best hope for the human species. His 1945 book, *The Perennial Philosophy,* gave impetus to what came to be known as the human-potential movement.

To many New Age communities, the human-potential movement has become an article of faith. They believe that by elevating their consciousness to levels previously unattained, they can generate energy that will break down the walls between mind and body, between Eastern wisdom and Western action, between the individual and society, and create, in Teilhard's phrase, a "persistent and irreversible rise of Cerebration and Consciousness."

Intentional communities have a deep and abiding faith that through their collective consciousness they can transform the world. A California community writes that such places are all-important in order to show "that humankind is meant to work out its problems together—that we are not separate, but part of the whole. Indeed, if we are to survive as a planet, we may have to learn this lesson on oneness—that our every action has an impact on the entire universe."

Oneness, the whole: Within those words lies the concept of holism, by which far-flung utopian communities are, despite their disparities, bound together in a unifying vision. Holism holds that the entire universe—each thing, atoms, individuals, communities, and galaxies as yet unseen—is made up of complete systems, or wholes. At the heart of holism is the conviction that the well-being of the planet depends on harmony between all living things and all matter. For the individual, holism entails the achievement of physical, mental, emotional, and spiritual balance and equilibrium with life, society, and nature. In more sweeping terms, holism means that only as the strands of a single, complex web can persons, communities, society, and the entirety of nature be understood.

Nowhere is the holistic oneness more highly developed than at a community in the village of Findhorn, on the

northeast coast of Scotland. The Findhorn group's founding came about in a strange way. In 1957, Peter and Eileen Caddy, an English couple, were hired to operate the 150-bed Cluny Hill Hotel, four miles from Findhorn. For five years, they ran the establishment according to precepts transmitted to Eileen by what she described as "the voice of God within." Under their stewardship, the hotel won a four-star rating and trebled its receipts. The owners, however, evidently were uncomfortable with that managerial style, and in 1962 the couple lost their jobs.

To Peter and Eileen, the setback was only a step toward fulfillment of a "larger plan or destiny." Now, Eileen's inner voice instructed the Caddys to live with their three small sons in a commercial trailer park located near a Findhorn garbage dump. Eileen was further told that the family should plant a garden and elevate their "vibrational level" by gorging themselves on its produce. Assisting in the endeavor would be Dorothy Maclean, an old friend and "spiritual coworker," who had been dismissed from the same hotel and who soon moved into the Caddys' trailer.

By her later account, Maclean was in "telepathic contact with the angelic Beings who overlight and direct plant growth." Known in Hinduism as devas—from the Sanskrit word for shining ones—those life-force spirits provided specific advice as to the care preferred by each of the garden's plant species. Still, neither Eileen Caddy's guiding voice nor Dorothy Maclean's devas would have sufficed to make a garden grow on the barren patch of land. In the lore of Islam's mystical Sufis (which Maclean had studied), there is a proverb: "Trust God—and tether your camel." At the Findhorn Foundation, accordingly, the spiritual was combined with the practical. With generous applications of horse manure, peat moss, lime, soot, and seaweed, the Findhorn garden flourished in sand and yielded vegetables and flowers so large and plentiful that they would have been extraordinary even under ideal gardening conditions. Visitors were flabbergasted, for instance, by the sight of cabbages weighing as much as forty-two pounds.

As word of the little enterprise spread, a number of similarly inclined people joined in. They began to regard themselves as an intentional community whose members specialized in communicating with the plants of the soil and the creatures of the field. "I found myself in the habit of talking with plants and animals," a Findhorn woman named Lida Sims recalled. "Often it would seem that I would get a response, for example, if I was thanking a plant for looking particularly beautiful. Sometimes it would seem to be words, but more often it was just a return of energy."

Once, taking a break from work, Sims was resting in a nearby grove of young white pines when she became aware of a surrounding sense of "agitation and upset. Suddenly I realized it was the trees." Sims had been operating a gasoline-powered tiller, and she thought that the trees were "worried because I was digging so close to where they were, and was I going to dig them up?" After Sims apologized and assured the trees that she had no such intention, they "seemed to be whispering, passing on what I had said from one end of the grove to the other and commenting on it. The pine grove then seemed satisfied and relaxed."

During one worrisome period, the group's vegetable gardens were infested by rabbits, moles, and a fungal disease called clubroot on the cabbage and other brassica vegetables. After standing in a circle and holding hands in silent attunement, the Findhornians, as one of them remembered, "communicated to the rabbits that they were welcome in the garden if they stayed on the grass banks and ate the clover and wildflower there. We asked the moles to leave the garden completely because their presence was too disruptive, but we did suggest an alternative place for them to go." The rabbits stayed and behaved themselves, while the moles apparently departed. As for the clubroot organisms, they were still "on all the brassicas," said the Findhornian, "and yet the plants grew anyway. The prevailing belief is that brassicas with clubroot can't grow into healthy specimens, but our cabbages disproved that." In truth, Findhorn's forty-pound cabbages soon became something of a tourist attraction.

But Findhorn's cadre was still minuscule. By 1970, after eight years, there were only twenty residents. In that year, a catalyst arrived in the person of David Spangler, a twenty-five-year-old American who had studied biochemistry and genetics at Arizona State University and later conducted an adult education course in esoteric and New Age philosophy in San Jose, California. Spangler had intended to drop in on Findhorn for a five-day visit; he stayed three years. His prolific writings—which, he said, were the literal rendering of transmissions from a source called Limitless Love and Truth—helped refine Findhorn's philosophy.

In their simplest terms, Spangler's concepts are embodied in a Findhorn creed: "Humankind is holy. Everything is unity." To Spangler, the oneness of God and humanity is crucial. Contrary to the traditional Judeo-Christian view of a transcendent God, separate in his majesty and approachable only through ritual, sacrifice, and prayer, Spangler held that God is one with humanity and that both are one with the earth and the cosmos.

Oneness with God is the start of a process of creating new things that Spangler called manifestation. "At Findhorn," he wrote, "the need is announced, thanks to God are given that the need is already met, and the community goes ahead, knowing that indeed the need has been met. In this way buildings have been constructed, printing presses purchased, other equipment and materials acquired without any money beforehand to pay for them. Whenever a need arises and is made known, it is always met in the right and perfect manner, often in a seemingly miraculous way."

By the time Spangler left, Findhorn had changed—not least in the roles played by its three founders. In 1972, Eileen Caddy emerged from a meditation to declare that while she would remain active at Findhorn, her inner voice would no longer advise the community. Her final spirit-inspired message to Findhornians was, "Go within and get your own guidance." Similarly, Dorothy Maclean's devas gradually faded from prominence, and in 1973 she was part of a group of Findhornians who moved to California's Bay Area to conduct conferences and workshops on holism.

As a former Royal Air Force officer, Peter Caddy had executed the directives from Eileen's and Dorothy's spirits with a brisk authority that sometimes grated on Findhornian sensitivities. In 1980, Peter left Findhorn—and Eileen— to live first in Hawaii and then in California with a new wife and child. (For reasons that baffle the foundation's residents, Findhorn's divorce rate has always been high, amounting at one point to 50 percent of all married couples within two years of their arrival.)

Meanwhile, Findhorn's membership grew to about 300 in 1978 before settling back down to around 200 in the less yeasty 1980s. Over the years, the community has branched into a variety of commercial enterprises—weaving, turning recycled paper into building insulation, and operating a publishing firm, a greeting-card business, and shops that sell books, handicraft items, health food, and toiletries. There also is the Garden School, which teaches modern horticultural techniques that do not rely on communing with devas; its facilities include a polyethylene tunnel with drip irrigation and subsoil solar heating.

Using the income from such ventures, along with loans and donations from benefactors, Findhorn has expanded its property holdings. The community has bought the Cluny Hill Hotel, which had fallen into disrepair after the Caddys departed, along with an old Findhorn railroad station and several mansions, which have been turned into classrooms, inns, and guesthouses. There is also Universal Hall, a pentagonal building that can seat 300 persons for cultural events and conferences. And a handful of Findhorn members live on and manage Erraid Island, a wind-swept, treeless island off Scotland's west coast. Here community members raise goats and retreat for purposes of contemplation.

Yet for all the material changes, oneness remains the prevailing spirit at Findhorn. The community makes its decisions not by decree but by a process of attunement, in which members hold hands, close their eyes, and experience a holistic coming together. To believers, it seems effective. As a Findhornian once said: "This is the best place I know where in a group setting we can help each person to contribute positively to the energy flow moving in the same direction. And love is what makes it all work."

Findhorn's loving energy also reaches outward. "Part of our work at Findhorn," said community member Ralph White, is to link up with other centers "to reveal an emerging pattern that we call the 'network of Light.'" Among the pen pals of the do-it-now community at Findhorn is a settlement in southern India, where time is reckoned by the passing of ages.

For more than 10,000 pilgrims who gathered on a bleak plateau near Pondicherry on February 28, 1968, the sun that rose blazing over the Bay of Bengal betokened the dawn of a new day for humankind. They had come from around the world to witness the birth of Auroville—The City of Dawn—taking place with the blessings of the United Nations Educational, Social, and Cultural Organization (UNESCO). They raised clouds of dust as they thronged into bleachers encircling a lotus-shaped urn.

The crowd was reverent as Auroville's brief charter was read in fifteen languages. It began: "Auroville belongs to nobody in particular. Auroville belongs to humanity as a whole. But to live in Auroville one must be the willing servitor of the Divine Consciousness." And it ended: "Auroville will be a site of material and spiritual researches for a living embodiment of an actual Human Unity."

When the observance ended, most of the visitors departed to pursue their own dreams in their own lands. But some remained, and they immediately set to work drilling wells and planting trees in soil so sunbaked that crowbars were required to break the surface. These were the pioneer inhabitants of a city planned as a utopian home for 50,000 persons, the willing servitors who would transform a vision into a reality. That vision was the product of spiritual union between a tough-minded woman of mystical bent and an Indian revolutionary turned guru.

The woman, Mirra Alfassa, was born in Paris in 1878, to a Turkish banker and his Egyptian wife. From her earliest years, Mirra was moved by strange forces. At the age of four, she later recounted, "There was a small chair for me on which I used to sit still, engrossed in my meditation. I would feel a sort of very pleasant

sensation of something very strong and very luminous, above my head—Consciousness. And my feeling was: this is what I must live, what I must be." Later, the presence took form as none less than Krishna—in the Hindu faith, one of the Divine Incarnations—and the girl was even able to draw a sketch of him.

As a young woman, Mirra moved in both artistic and occult circles. She was married twice, first to a Parisian painter and later to Paul Richard, a French diplomat with an interest in Eastern spirituality. In 1910, Richard traveled to Pondicherry, then a French protectorate, on a political matter. While there, he sought out a guru by the name of Sri (meaning "venerated") Aurobindo, to inquire about the symbolic meaning of the Star of David. (This was the same Aurobindo in whose ashram Esalen Institute's Michael Murphy later meditated.) The two men became friendly, and when Richard returned to Pondicherry several years later, he brought his wife and introduced her to Sri Aurobindo—whom she tells us she instantly recognized as being the Krishna of her visions.

From that moment on, Mirra had no doubt about

Blending the traditional with the New Age, Findhornians gather around a candle for a Christmas Eve "angel" meditation. "We release the 'angel' we have had with us for the previous year," explained a resident, "and choose an 'angel' or quality that will be our overlighting focus for the coming year."

where she belonged. After the meeting she wrote in her diary: "An immense gratitude rises from my heart. I seem to have at last arrived at the threshold which I have long sought." Paul Richard later bowed out gracefully, going so far as to pay tribute to Sri Aurobindo's towering superiority. "Around mountain peaks there can be only valleys," he said. "I have no wish to be a valley."

The yogi into whose esoteric sphere Mirra now moved was born in Calcutta in 1872. Aurobindo Ghose, the son of an Anglophilic Indian physician who took to drink and of a mother who eventually descended into madness, was educated in England. As a classical scholar at Cambridge, he was fluent in Latin before he became familiar with his native tongue. After Cambridge, Ghose found employment with the maharaja of Baroda, who had taken a fancy to him while visiting London. Thus, in 1893, Ghose returned to the homeland where he would spend the rest of his life. For thirteen years, he languished in a series of clerical jobs in the princely state of Baroda—and found relief from the tedium by involving himself in the cause of Indian independence. In those early days of the movement, when young Mohandas K. Gandhi was still off practicing law in South Africa, most Indian nationalists believed that Great Britain could be persuaded to grant freedom through peaceful negotiation. Aurobindo Ghose, however, was not so trusting; he left the maharaja's service to hurl the firebrand of revolutionary violence.

Aurobindo had a way with a pen, and he soon became editor of *Bande Mataram,* the journal of Indian nationalism's so-called extremist faction. Urging rebellion against the colonial government, he naturally drew unfavorable British attention, and in 1908 the Raj managed to jail him. Aurobindo spent nearly a year in solitary confinement, and in the silence of his cell he began having visions. "I lay on the coarse blankets that were given me for a couch," he wrote later, "and felt the arms of Sri Krishna around me, the arms of my Friend and Lover." Even before his incarceration, Aurobindo had delved into yoga. Now it became his life's focus—and the philosophical underpinning for the future utopian community of Auroville.

Yoga generally calls for a renunciation of secular life. In that sense, the discipline Aurobindo chose was distinctly different. It is called karma-yoga—the "yoga of action." As explained by Aurobindo, "the spiritual life finds its most potent expression in the man who lives the ordinary life of men in the strength of Yoga." Years later, Mirra Alfassa would offer to the citizens of Auroville a succinct corollary. "All work," she said, "is a kind of communion."

It was thus in harmony with his yoga that Aurobindo, after his release from jail, resumed his political activities—but not for long. Harassed by British authorities, he received an *adesh*—a divine command—telling him to seek sanctuary in French-controlled Pondicherry. From there, in 1910, came a letter to a Madras newspaper saying that Sri Auro-

A predawn bonfire (left) dimly illuminates a crowd of Auroville residents gathered on February 28, 1988, to commemorate the twentieth anniversary of the utopian community on the southeastern coast of India. Silhouetted against the newly forested horizon is the spherical shape of the Matrimandir, under construction since 1971 and meant to serve as Auroville's spiritual center. Its name means "temple of the mother."

bindo wished to "see and correspond with no one in connection with political subjects." Instead, he wrote, he hoped that he could continue his spiritual studies undistracted by worldly turmoil.

By 1920, when Mirra Alfassa moved into his household, Sri Aurobindo had attracted a handful of young followers who lived in contented disarray. Mirra soon began setting things straight, stacking the books neatly in cupboards, planting a small kitchen garden, organizing collective meditations, and even assigning to Sri Aurobindo the task of cooking fish for her cats. At first, to be sure, there were grumbles from the

disciples. But they were silenced when Sri Aurobindo announced that Mirra was the earthly representation of Shakti, the Divine Mother, whose spiritual knowledge was "predominatingly practical in its nature." That being the case, it was the Mother—as she would henceforth be known—who would lead the acolytes through the daily disciplines of yoga while Sri Aurobindo withdrew ever deeper into his meditations.

His philosophy differed from traditional Indian thought. He could not agree that the material world is mere illusion, to be spurned in pursuit of bliss. He insisted that the world is the real manifestation of the Godhead. "You need not give up the world," he declared, "in order to advance in self-realization." But human beings are evolving, he stated, toward higher consciousness, a life as far beyond humanity as humanity is beyond the monkey. He viewed the crises he saw in the world as evidence that this evolutionary leap was beginning, that the old ways of thinking would no longer solve problems. He looked forward to

A red cement sculpture (above) adorns the entrance to the community's school, built in 1971. It was named Last School, perhaps in the hope that Auroville could one day do without formal education.

The marble Lotus Urn at near left, centerpiece of the amphitheater, symbolizes Auroville's creation as an international community. At the founding ceremony, children from 124 nations placed handfuls of their countries' soil in the urn.

"a spiritualized society," which would live "not as the collective ego, but as the collective soul."

Under the Mother's management, what had been a small study group became a full-fledged ashram, or Hindu religious community, that numbered some 1,200 residents by the time Sri Aurobindo died in 1950. Although the Mother would remain at the ashram for the rest of her life, her thoughts in the years after the loss of her mentor turned increasingly toward establishing a place for "all who aspire to live the Truth of tomorrow." It would be named Auroville. As envisioned by the Mother, Auroville would become a laboratory for developing the new consciousness, a place where people "can live away from all national rivalries, social conventions, self-contradictory moralities and contending religions." The community would welcome, she said, the help of "all those who find that the world is not as it ought to be."

In the spirit of Sri Aurobindo's karma-yoga, ideas were the wellspring of deeds. "No words—acts!" the Mother admonished her followers. And so she set to work, drawing plans and founding an organization—it was called the Sri Aurobindo Society, and she was its president—to raise money and acquire land. It was a slow process, and not until the opening ceremony was held on that memorable morning of 1968 did Auroville begin to take visible form.

A model of the City of Dawn, when viewed from above, appeared as a spiral galaxy, with broad avenues spinning outward in symmetry. At the center was a huge golden sphere named the Matrimandir, a meditation center that would be, in the Mother's words, "the soul of Auroville." The structure, which measured almost 100 feet by 120 feet, would be supported by four arching pillars representing the Mother's four powers: Maheshwari (Wisdom), Mahalaksmi (Strength), Mahasarawati (Harmony), and Mahakali (Perfection). The top half of the sphere would be a twelve-sided Inner Chamber, its walls lined with forty tons of white marble. From atop the edifice, a sun-tracking mirror would deflect the sun's rays to an enormous, clear crystal globe, which would illuminate the sanctuary.

Surrounding the Matrimandir at a distance of about two miles would be the Green Belt—hardwood forests, orchards of mango, cashew, and other fruit and nut trees, and twelve gardens luxuriant with hibiscuses and orchids. In all, Auroville would be contained within a 12,000-acre circle. Of

that, however, only some 2,000 acres would be occupied by Aurovilians, in settlements bearing such names as Aspiration, Peace, Certitude, and Utility. Much of the remaining land would rest with 20,000 Tamil tribesmen; Auroville's venturers into the New Age would be living cheek by jowl with a people still practicing the customs of their ancestors of 2,000 years before.

Hard reality set in early. The day after the 1968 ceremony, one of the original residents surveyed the surroundings and was shocked at what he saw. "It was empty," he recalled later. "It was wind-blown. There wasn't a tree. There was nothing." In the months that followed, a cruel sun bore down on the settlers as they labored to create their new home. The Tamil natives, whom the Aurovilians had expected to be friendly companions on the voyage into humanity's future, turned out to be distinctly suspicious. As one Tamil later recalled, "The first Aurovilians came to the village in jeeps. They gave sweets. We thought they were trying to take our land, to chase us away."

Yet despite all these difficulties, the early Aurovilians adhered to the discipline of karma-yoga and worked with a vigor that was born of their vision. Reforestation began. The foundation stone for the Matrimandir was laid on February 21, 1971.

And then, on November 17, 1973, Auroville suffered a stunning loss: The Mother, in the Hindu phrase, left her body at age ninety-five. Her death left the community leaderless and brought considerable turmoil, but Auroville survived and kept building. By 1990, more than two million trees had been planted; erosion had slowed, water had returned to the ancient dry wells of the Tamil villages, and songbirds could be heard in the new forests. Work on the Inner Chamber of the Matrimandir was almost done, although the entire edifice was several years from completion. Auroville still depended largely on donations from friends around the world for its continued existence, but a

The mushroom-shaped buildings at left house the library of Auroville's Last School, and the pyramids in the background contain a science lab. This photograph was taken in 1972, soon after the structures were built; they now enjoy shade from some of the million trees Aurovilians have planted. At right, in the settlement of Ami, an artist's home typifies the inventiveness seen in Auroville.

In a Last School classroom, children of Auroville learn Sanskrit. The schools also teach French, English, and Tamil, the indigenous language. Regarding education as a chance to evolve a new kind of person, Auroville's teachers embrace unorthodox teaching methods, such as using all of Auroville as a classroom and consulting the children on subject matter as well as teaching methods.

variety of cottage industries had sprung up.

In one settlement, for example, Aurovilians applied Western marketing techniques to the sale of products woven by traditional Tamil methods; not far away, a community of skilled Germans and French manufactured microcomputers. Of Auroville's 725 residents, about two-thirds were Westerners, with Europeans greatly outnumbering Americans. Most of the rest were Indians, and to the gratification of the Aurovilians who had once been considered intruders, about 2,500 Tamil villagers were working in the community's various businesses or joining in its educational and training programs. Auroville had recently hosted its own international citizen diplomacy project, bringing together forty-five young adults, fifteen each from India, the Soviet Union, and the United States, for two weeks of cultural exchange and tree planting. And the community enjoyed the recognition and support of the Indian government, conferred on it in 1988 by a special act of the Indian Parliament.

Living conditions varied greatly among Auroville's forty or more scattered settlements. Near the center of the community were neighborhoods that a former Aurovilian from Germany compared to "a suburb of Frankfurt."

Buckminster Fuller's Vision: Doing More with Less

R. Buckminster Fuller (below) strove to create an earthly utopia through ingenious design and engineering. By doing more with less, he believed, "we could take care of everybody." Born in 1895, when horses were common and light bulbs exotic, Fuller was largely self-taught. His World War I navy service and a succession of jobs gave him a solid technological base but left him penniless. In 1927, suicidal over business failures, he suddenly found himself lifted from a Chicago sidewalk "in a sparkling kind of sphere" and heard a voice tell him never to wait for "temporal attestation to your thought. You think the truth." Believing that "we're here for each other," Fuller set out to invent his way to utopia.

In 1928, he unveiled a design for a portable home (below). Called the Dymaxion house, it hung from a central mast and was meant to be mass-produced and delivered by air for one-fifth the cost of the average home. It never reached mass production, but another Fuller invention did: the geodesic dome. Using as his basic building blocks tetrahedrons (shapes with four flat sides) made from simple struts, Fuller created hollow hemispheres that provided immense strength from minimal building materials. His geodesic domes were put into use all over the world.

Few of his notions won such acceptance, but he was not dismayed. "My ideas," he said, "have undergone a process of emergence by emergency. When they are needed badly enough, they're accepted."

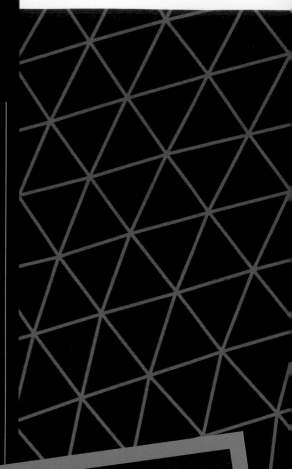

In an artist's conception, the plastic-covered geodesic dome Fuller envisioned to shelter central Manhattan stretches across the width of the island and from Twenty-Second Street to Sixty-Second Street, rising three-quarters of a mile above the Empire State Building. A dome this size would contain less steel than the Queen Mary. Fuller said the controlled climate within it would save not only fuel but cleaning costs.

Fuller's proposed Cloud Nines—futuristic lighter-than-air machines—float across an earth landscape, using the cost-free energy of the sun. A plastic-covered geodesic sphere half a mile in diameter, Fuller calculated, would weigh only one one-thousandth as much as the air within it and would rise when the sun warmed that air. Each sphere, he said, could provide transportation or habitation for thousands of people.

Pictured riding at anchor above San Francisco Bay is another of Fuller's later concepts, a city within a tetrahedronal pyramid that floats on air. Like the Cloud Nine, the city would depend on solar heating to levitate it. Fuller believed his sky-riding structures, domed cities, and lightweight air-delivered housing would provide cheap shelter for all without depleting the earth's resources.

There, the residents of attractive modern homes enjoyed one of southern India's most valued conveniences—running water. On Auroville's outer fringes, other residents chose to dwell in simple huts and used community-built windmills to draw their water from wells. But creature comforts have never held a high place among Auroville's priorities, and the mortar and marble of homes and public buildings rank far below attunement with the environment and the attainment of human harmony. Says one Aurovilian: "We have to get it together to take care of the whole Auroville watershed, to complete reforestation and water management work. We have to expand our consciousness over the whole plateau."

Then, almost as an afterthought, he adds: "Oh! And yes, we have to start the city."

Esalen, Findhorn, and Auroville: The three communities present different scenes, different missions, different views of their place on the planet. Intentional communities offer a vast variety to the world they seek to change. Whereas Auroville is a new settlement in a desert wilderness, other intentional communities take up residence in existing cities. Some are content to see themselves simply as islands of tranquility amid the frantic urban hurly-burly. "We live on a noisy city street and come together for dinner every night, sharing our city adventures," announces San Francisco's New Moon House. "We are TV-free, mostly vegetarian and non-smoking." On New York's Staten Island, members of the Foundation for Feedback Learning own four adjacent houses, with land enough between them for flower and vegetable gardens and outdoor eating space. According to the group's literature, they "have six open porches and enough room to sit around and talk, play, party or just retreat, outdoors as well as in."

Other urban communities perform good works. In Milwaukee, Casa Maria was founded in 1967 by a group of Catholics who "saw the need of the Catholic Church to become more involved in helping the poor on the streets." In addition to providing food, clothing, and used furniture to

the poor, Casa Maria owns a house large enough to take in four families and three single women. Still other intentional communities undertake charitable projects that require considerable capital outlay. "Dream big," is a motto of the Gesundheit Institute of Arlington, Virginia. After twelve years of living together and delivering health-care services to some 15,000 persons, Gesundheit members turned to raising funds to build a hospital in West Virginia.

In the sense that such enterprises would have been beyond the wildest imaginings of the flower children of the 1960s and 1970s, they reflect a growing maturity. "As individuals and communities, many of us have left behind our childish reactionary tendencies," comments David Thatcher, a product of the sixties, whose 100 Mile House in British Columbia is part of the Emissary Foundation International, which operates approximately 200 intentional communities for perhaps 10,000 people on six continents. "We no longer speak of ourselves as an 'alternative society,' " Thatcher continues, "but as 'complementary catalysts' or 'centers of light.' "

Some New Age groups operate along lines that many more conventional institutions might envy. The Federation of Egalitarian Communities, for example, is a network of six organizations from Oregon to New Hampshire and Ontario, whose 200 or so members together gross about one million dollars a year from various cottage industries. All six have existed for more than ten years, and from their collective experience the federation has compiled a portfolio including membership agreements, bylaws, property and behavior codes, labor and governance systems, statements of philosophy, tax-status documents, and visitor policies. Members who travel from one community to another to work or participate in conferences receive subsidies, and a fund is maintained to protect against large medical bills.

David Thatcher also notes that many communities "are shifting their approach from one of confrontation to one of respecting and working with existing authorities." The Roandoak of God Christian Commune at Morro Bay,

California, provides work therapy to troubled persons who have been sent there by probation officials and churches. Christmas Star, a community in Winkelman, Arizona, offers archery, firearm, and survival courses and proudly reports that it maintains a ''congenial relationship with law enforcement officers.''

New Age groups have come a long way from the days when communes were incubators of the drug culture. It has become common for intentional communities to ban illegal drugs as well as alcohol and tobacco. Still, by their very nature, many communities alarm conventional neighbors. Communities of homosexuals, for instance, sometimes meet scorn from the local populace. Yet the gays not only hold their ground but sometimes take the offensive on behalf of their causes. Thus the ''wimmin,'' as they call themselves, of Spiral, a lesbian community in Monticello, Kentucky, say they are dedicated to ''promoting feminism and challenging sexism, racism, ageism, ablism, capitalism, and heterosexism in our patriarchal society.''

The umbrella of the New Age spreads wide over scores of communities with missions as varied as the imagination, from presenting theatrical performances in rural Canadian towns to communing with dolphins in the far Pacific. A publication of San Francisco's Kerista Commune asserts that, ''If you had to sum up what we're trying to do in one sentence, you could say that we want to make the world safe for rock 'n roll.'' In spiritual beliefs and practices, New Agers range along a rainbow of hues. Many of them live in simple, nondenominational Christianity. Others have more formal ties: The Holy City Community, which is situated on sixty acres of swampy Louisiana woodland, is subject to the authority of a Catholic bishop; in Berkeley, California, members of the Aquarian Minyan describe themselves as an ''egalitarian Jewish spiritual community'' and meet as a mobile synagogue in one another's homes. Some communities do not have any orthodox ties. Near Perth, Australia, members of a community that calls itself the Universal Brotherhood preach that Jesus of Nazareth is the commander of a fleet of Unidentified Flying Objects whose occupants patrol the planet and act as ''elder brothers'' to earthlings.

But it is in the exploration of Eastern religions, philosophies, disciplines, and mysteries that countless intentional communities aspire to expand their consciousness and thereby generate globe-changing energies. Gurus abound, bearing such names as Swami Amar Jyodi, Prabhushri Swamji, and Lord Caitanya Mahaprabhu. Following the precepts of such mentors, communities around the world study Vedic texts, Buddha dharma, and Krishna consciousness; they practice the disciplines of kundalini yoga, tantric yoga, bhakti yoga, karma-yoga, hatha-yoga, and Zen Buddhism.

nd then there are the farms, scores if not hundreds of them, dotting the rolling English countryside, the foothills of the Pyrenees, the forbidding Australian outback, the velds of Africa, and the valleys of Oregon. Some possess well over 2,000 acres; others are tiny patches. Some are high-tech operations with photovoltaic electricity, drip irrigation and solar-powered pumping systems, hydroponic greenhouses, and computerized planting schedules. At others, the land is tilled with horse-drawn plows, and indoor plumbing is a triumph. Yet no matter what their size or degree of sophistication, the farming communities are sustained by an age-old human yearning to attain a oneness with the land and to watch plants come to life.

Whatever their leaning, style, or direction, all intentional communities are bent on creating a better world. For some, that world is personal, for some it is local, but for many it is also planetary. ''Scattered around the Earth,'' said one Findhornian, ''are untold thousands of individuals, small groups and communities quietly creating a society based upon the unity of the human family and co-creation with the forces of nature.'' To Corinne McLaughlin and Gordon Davidson, who visited more than a hundred of them in writing a book on the subject, such communities contain ''an unmistakable optimism and vitality that you seldom find in mainstream society.'' In this ''enthusiasm and creativity,'' they said, they found nothing less than ''the energy of the future visiting the present.''

ACKNOWLEDGMENTS

The editors wish to thank the following: Stefania Auroli, Rome; Lydia Bonora, Relations Publiques, Musée des Beaux Arts, Chartres, France; Kathryn Booth, Terre Nouvelle, Laragne, France; Caroline Bourbonnais, La Fabuloserie, Dicy, France; the Center for Communal Studies, University of Southern Indiana, Evansville, Indiana; Ester Coen, Rome; Dr. Bodo von Dewitz, Agfa Foto-Historama, Cologne, West Germany; Professor Robert Fogarty, Antioch College, Yellow Springs, Ohio; Jerry Grant, Shaker Museum; Sabine Hartmann, Bauhaus-Archiv, West Berlin; Kansas Grassroots Art Association, Lawrence, Kansas; Monika Kinley, Outsider Archive, London; Heidi Klein, Bildarchiv Preussischer Kulturbesitz, West Berlin; Susanne Klingeberg, Itzehoe, West Germany; Grace Knoche, the Theosophical Society; Robert Knodt, Fotografische Sammlung im Museum Folkwang, Essen, West Germany; Martina de Luca, Rome; G. Franco Maffina, Director, Fondazione Russolo-Pratella, Varese, Italy; June Maher, Auroville International USA, Sacramento, California; Kirby van Mater, the Theosophical Society; Jean Prince, Findhorn Foundation, Forres, Scotland; Michele del Re, Rome; Father Ronald, the Brotherhood of the Essenes, Seven Oaks, Kent, England; C. Raman Schlemmer, Curator of Oskar Schlemmer Family Estate and Oskar Schlemmer Theater Estate, Oggebbio, Italy; SPACES (Saving and Preserving Arts and Cultural Environments), Los Angeles; Roberto Sparagio, Comunità Damanhur, Baldissero Canavese, Turin, Italy; Sergio Slingo, Milan, Italy; Lise Tatin, Musée Robert Tatin, Cossé-le-Vivien, France; Achim Windschuh, Akademic der Künste, Abt. Baukunst, West Berlin.

BIBLIOGRAPHY

Adams, Steven, *Arts & Crafts Movement*. Secaucus, N.J.: Chartwell, 1987.

Andô, Shôei, *Zen and American Transcendentalism*. Tokyo: Hokuseido Press, 1970.

Andrews, Edward D.:
The Gift to Be Simple. New York: Dover, 1962.
The People Called Shakers. New York: Dover, 1963.

Apollonio, Umbro, ed., *Futurist Manifestos*. Transl. by Robert Brain et al. New York: Viking, 1973.

Auroville Today (Tamil Nadu, India), February 28, 1989, and August-September 1989.

The Avant Garde in Russia: 1910-1930 (exhibition catalog). Los Angeles: Los Angeles County Museum of Art, 1986.

Bayer, Herbert, Walter Gropius, and Ise Gropius, *Bauhaus 1919-1928*. New York: Museum of Modern Art, 1938.

Bell, Quentin, *Ruskin*. New York: George Braziller, 1978.

Benesch, Otto, *The Art of the Renaissance in Northern Europe*. Greenwich, Conn.: Phaidon, 1965.

Bennett, J. G.: *Gurdjieff: Making a New World*. London: Turnstone, 1973.

Berneri, Marie Louise, *Journey through Utopia*. Freeport, N.Y.: Books for Libraries Press, 1969.

Bestor, Arthur Eugene, Jr., *Backwood Utopias*. Philadelphia: University of Pennsylvania Press, 1950.

Biesantz, Hagen, and Arne Klingborg, *The Goetheanum*. London: Rudolf Steiner Press, 1979.

Boller, P. F., Jr., *American Transcendentalism, 1830-1860*. New York: G. P. Putnam's Sons, 1974.

Brewer, Priscilla J., *Shaker Communities, Shaker Lives*. Hanover, N.H.: University Press of New England, 1986.

Canaday, John, *Mainstreams of Modern Art*. New York: Holt, Rinehart and Winston, 1964.

Carden, Maren Lockwood, *Oneida: Utopian Community to Modern Corporation*. Baltimore: Johns Hopkins Press, 1969.

Carmean, E. A., Jr., *Mondrian: The Diamond Compositions*. Washington, D.C.: National Gallery of Art, 1979.

Chelminski, Rudolph, "Robert Tatin—Artist, Fantasist, Visionary—Revels in Museum Built with His Own, and His Wife's, Hands." *Smithsonian*, February 1979.

Cheney, Sheldon, *Men Who Have Walked with God*. New York: Alfred A. Knopf, 1946.

Chevalier, Denys, *Klee.*. Transl. by Eileen B. Hennessey. New York: Crown, 1979.

Collins, George R., *Antonio Gaudí*. New York: George Braziller, 1960.

Comstock, Craig, and Gordon Feller, "New Wave Diplomat." *Nuclear Times*, November-December 1986.

Corcoran, Bobbi, *The New Age Community Guidebook*. Middletown, Calif.: Harbin Springs, 1988.

Covello, Joe, and Lowell Benedict, "Clarence Schmidt." *Cosmopolitan*, December 1964.

Crease, Robert, and Charles Mann, "The Transformed Trash of Untrained Artists." *Smithsonian*, August 1983.

Curtis, Edith Roelker, *A Season in Utopia*. New York: Russell & Russell, 1961.

Descharnes, Robert, and Clovis Prévost, *Gaudi: The Visionary*. New York: Dorset Press, 1982.

Easton, Stewart C., *Rudolf Steiner: Herald of a New Epoch*. Spring Valley, N.Y.: Anthroposophic Press, 1980.

Edwards, Paul, ed., *The Encyclopedia of Philosophy*. Vol. 7. New York: Macmillan, 1967.

Eliade, Mircea:
The Myth of the Eternal Return. Transl. by Willard R. Trask. Princeton, N.J.: Princeton University Press, 1954.
The Sacred and the Profane. Transl. by Willard R. Trask. San Diego: Harcourt Brace Jovanovich, 1959.

Eliade, Mircea, ed., *The Encyclopedia of Religion*. Vols. 6 and 11. New York: Macmillan, 1987.

The Encyclopedia of Eastern Philosophy and Religion. Boston: Shambhala, 1989.

Fauchereau, Serge, ed., *Moscow 1900-1930*. New York: Rizzoli, 1988.

Ferguson, John:
Encyclopedia of Mysticism and Mystery Religions. New York: Crossroad, 1982.
Utopias of the Classical World. Ithaca, N.Y.: Cornell University Press, 1975.

Ferguson, Marilyn, *The Aquarian Conspiracy*. Los Angeles: J. P. Tarcher, 1980.

The Findhorn Community:
Faces of Findhorn. San Francisco: Harper & Row, 1980.
The Findhorn Garden. San Francisco: Harper & Row, 1975.

Finster, Howard, as told to Tom Patterson, *Howard Finster: Stranger from Another World*. New York: Abbeville Press, 1989.

Fletcher, John, *Art Inspired by Rudolf Steiner*. Hertfordshire, England: Mercury Arts, 1987.

Fletcher, Valerie J., *Nightmares: Utopian Visions in Modern Art*. Washington, D.C.: Smithsonian Institution Press, 1983.

Franciscono, Marcel, *Walter Gropius and the Creation of the Bauhaus in Weimar*. Urbana, Ill.: University of Illinois, 1971.

Friedman, Mildred, ed., *De Stijl: 1917-1931 Visions of Utopia* (exhibition catalog). New York: Abbeville Press, 1982.

"From Foundation to Foundation." *Auroville Today* (Tamil Nandu, India), February 28, 1989.

Fuller, R. Buckminster, *Critical Path*. New York: St. Martin's Press, 1981.

Gaines, Judith, "In the Eden of Id." *The Boston Globe Magazine*, June 21, 1987.

Gardner, Albert TenEyck, and Stuart P. Feld, *American Paintings* (exhibition catalog). New York: Metropolitan Museum of Art, 1965.

Gaunt, William, *The Pre-Raphaelite Dream*. New York: Schoken Books, 1966.

Genovese, E. N., "Paradise and Golden Age: Ancient Origins of the Heavenly Utopia." *The Utopian Vision*. San Diego: San Diego State University Press, 1983.

Glenn, Jerome Clayton:
"Auroville." *The Futurist*, October 1980.
Linking the Future: Findhorn, Auroville, Arcosanti. Cambridge, Mass.: Hexiad Project, 1979.
"Prototype Communities of Tomorrow: Auroville." *The Futurist*, October 1980.

Greenwald, Jeff, "Glasnost by the Bay." *San Francisco Focus*, December 1989.

Harvey, David, *Thorsons Complete Guide to Alternative Living*. Wellingborough, England: Thorsons, 1986.

Hawken, Paul, *The Magic of Findhorn*. San Francisco: Harper & Row, 1975.

Hayden, Dolores, *Seven American Utopias*. Cambridge, Mass.: MIT Press, 1976.

Heehs, Peter, *Sri Aurobindo: A Brief Biography*. New York: Oxford University Press, 1989.

Heinberg, Richard:
Memories and Visions of Paradise. Los Angeles: Jeremy P. Tarcher, 1989.
"The Universal Myth of the Lost Golden Age." *New Realities*, May-June 1989.

Hemleben, Johannes, *Rudolf Steiner: A Documentary Biography*. Transl. by Leo Twyman. Sussex, England: Henry Goulden, 1975.

Hemphill, Herbert W., Jr., and Julia Weissman, *Twentieth-Century American Folk Art and Artists*. New York: E. P. Dutton, 1974.

Henderson, Philip, *William Morris: His Life, Work and Friends*. New York: McGraw-Hill, 1967.

Hertzler, Joyce Oramel, *The History of Utopian Thought*. New York: Macmillan, 1926.

Hilton, Timothy, *The Pre-Raphaelites*. New York: Harry N. Abrams, 1970.

Holloway, Mark, *Heavens on Earth*. New York: Dover, 1966.

Holme, Bryan, *Enchanted World: The Magic of Pictures*. London: Thames and Hudson, 1979.

Horgan, Edward R., *The Shaker Holy Land*. Harvard, Mass.: Harvard Common Press, 1982.

In the Image of Man: The Indian Perception of the Universe through 2000 Years of Painting and Sculpture. New York: Alpine Fine Arts Collection, 1982.

"In Long-Forbidden Tibet." *National Geographic*, February 1980.

Jones, Allen H., *Essenes*. Lanham, Md.: University Press of America, 1985.

de Jong, Casper, *Paintings of the Western World*. New York: Barnes & Noble, 1963.

Jouve, Jean-Pierre, Claude Prévost, and Clovis Prévost. *Le

Palais Idéal du Facteur Cheval. Paris: Moniteur, 1981.

Kagan, Donald, Steven Ozment, and Frank M. Turner, *The Western Heritage: 1300-1815*. New York: Macmillan, 1983.

Kahn, Alice, "Esalen at 25." *Los Angeles Times Magazine*, December 6, 1987.

Kanter, Rosebeth Moss:
Commitment and Community. Cambridge, Mass.: Harvard University Press, 1972.
Communes. San Francisco: Harper & Row, 1973.

Kephart, William M., *Extraordinary Groups*. New York: St. Martin's Press, 1982.

King, Ronald, *The Quest for Paradise: A History of the World's Gardens*. New York: Mayflower, 1979.

Kourik, Robert, "The Lessons of Esalen." *National Gardening*, January 1988.

Laidler, Harry W., *Social-Economic Movements*. New York: Thomas Y. Crowell, 1946.

Lamson, David R., *Two Years' Experience among the Shakers*. West Boylston, Mass.: David R. Lamson, 1848.

Larson, Martin A., *The Essene Heritage*. New York: Philosophical Library, 1967.

Leonard, George, "Encounters at the Mind's Edge." *Esquire*, June 1985.

Lipke, William C., and Gregg Blasdel, *Schmidt* (exhibition catalog). Burlington, Vt.: Robert Hull Fleming Museum, University of Vermont, 1975.

Litwak, Leo E., "Joy Is the Prize." *The New York Times Magazine*, December 31, 1967.

Lockridge, Ross F., *The Labyrinth*. Westport, Conn.: Hyperion Press, 1975.

Lohman, Ruud, *A House for the Third Millennium: Essays on Matrimandir*. Paris: Alain Grandcolas, no date.

McKnight, Floyd, *Rudolf Steiner and Anthroposophy*. New York: Anthroposophical Society in America, 1977.

McLaughlin, Corinne, and Gordon Davidson, *Builders of the Dawn: Community Lifestyles in a Changing World*. Shutesbury, Mass.: Sirius, 1986.

Manley, Roger, *Signs and Wonders: Outsider Art inside North Carolina* (exhibition catalog). Raleigh, N.C.: North Carolina Museum of Art, 1989.

Marshall, Tyler, "A Futuristic Community Fails." *Providence Rhode Island Evening Bulletin*, December 8, 1982.

Martin, Eddie Owens, as told to Tom Patterson, *St. Eom in the Land of Pasaquan*. The Jargon Society, Columbus, Ga., 1987.

May, Antoinette, "Auroville: Legacy of a Goddess." *Psychic*, September-October 1974.

Melton, J. Gordon, *Encyclopedia of American Religions*. Detroit: Gale Research, 1987.

Missing Pieces: Georgia Folk Art (exhibition catalog). Atlanta: Georgia Council for the Arts and Humanities, 1976.

Molnar, Thomas, *Utopia: The Perennial Heresy*. London: Tom Stacy, 1972.

Moment, Gairdner B., and Otto F. Kraushaar, eds., *Utopias: The American Experience*. Metuchen, N.J.: Scarecrow Press, 1960.

Moore, James, *Gurdjieff and Mansfield*. London: Routledge & Kegan Paul, 1980.

Morgan, Arthur E., *Nowhere Was Somewhere: How History Makes Utopias and How Utopias Make History*. Westport, Conn.: Greenwood Press, 1976.

Moszynska, Anna, *Abstract Art*. London: Thames and Hudson, 1990.

The Mother on Auroville. Auroville, Tamil Nandu, India: Auropublications, 1977.

Moynihan, Elizabeth B., *Paradise as a Garden: In Persia and Mughal India*. New York: George Braziller, 1979.

Mumford, Lewis, *The Story of Utopias*. Gloucester, Mass.: Peter Smith, 1959 (reprint of 1922 edition).

Naives and Visionaries (exhibition catalog). Walker Art Center, Minneapolis. New York: E. P. Dutton, 1974.

Naylor, Gillian, *The Bauhaus Reassessed: Sources and Design Theory*. New York: E. P. Dutton, 1985.

Naylor, Gillian, ed., *William Morris by Himself: Designs and Writings*. Boston: Little, Brown, 1988.

Newman, Cathy, "The Shakers' Brief Eternity." *National Geographic*, September 1989.

"The Next Challenge." *Auroville Today* (Tamil Nandu, India), February 28, 1989.

Nisbet, Robert, "America as Utopia." *Current*, June 1987.

Oxley, William, *Modern Messiahs and Wonder Workers*. London: Trübner, 1889.

Pérouse de Montclos, Jean-Marie, *Etienne-Louise Boullée (1728-1799)*. New York: George Braziller, 1974.

Plato, *The Republic*. Transl. by A. D. Lindsay. Franklin Center, Pa.: Franklin Library, 1975.

Popenoe, Oliver, and Cris Popenoe, *Seeds of Tomorrow: New Age Communities That Work*. San Francisco: Harper & Row, 1984.

Richards, I. A., ed., *The Republic of Plato*. New York: W. W. Norton, 1942.

Richardson, E. P., *Painting in America: From 1502 to the Present*. New York: Thomas Y. Crowell, 1965.

Rose, Anne C., *Transcendentalism as a Social Movement*. New Haven, Conn.: Yale University Press, 1981.

Rose, Milton C., and Emily Mason, eds., *A Shaker Reader*. New York: Universe Books, 1975.

Rosen, Seymour, "Environments in France." *SPACES*, Number 10, 1989.

Roters, Eberhard, *Painters of the Bauhaus*. New York: Frederick A. Praeger, 1969.

Rudofsky, Bernard, "Home Is What You Make It." *Horizon*, autumn 1964.

Ruedi, Hans, and Priska Clerc, *The Goetheanum and Its Surroundings*. Transl. by Ekkehard Piening. Dornach, Switzerland: Goetheanum Press, 1987.

Sasson, Diane, *The Shaker Spiritual Narrative*. Knoxville, Tenn.: University of Tennessee Press, 1983.

Scott-Kilvert, Ian, ed., *British Writers*. Vol. 7. New York: Charles Scribner's Sons, 1984.

Shambaugh, Bertha M. H., *Amana*. Iowa City, Iowa: State Historical Society of Iowa, 1988.

Sharp, Dennis, ed., *Glass Architecture by Paul Scheerbart and Alpine Architecture by Bruno Taut*. New York: Praeger, 1972.

Sieden, Lloyd Steven, *Buckminster Fuller's Universe*. New York: Plenum Press, 1989.

Snyder, Robert, ed., *Buckminster Fuller*. New York: St. Martin's Press, 1980.

de Solà-Morales, Ignasi, *Gaudi*. New York: Rizzoli, 1984.

Spangler, David:
Towards a Planetary Vision. Forres, Scotland: Findhorn Foundation, 1977.
Vision of Findhorn Anthology. Forres, Scotland: Findhorn Foundation, 1976.

Speeth, Kathleen Riordan, *The Gurdjieff Work*. Los Angeles: Jeremy P. Tarcher, 1989.

The Spiritual in Art: Abstract Painting 1890-1985 (exhibition catalog). New York: Abbeville Press, 1986.

Sri Aurobindo and the Mother, *Towards Tomorrow*. Pondicherry, India: Sri Aurobindo Society, 1974.

Steiner, Rudolf:
Colour. Transl. by John Salter. London: Rudolf Steiner Press, 1971.
The Essential Steiner. Ed. by Robert A. McDermott. San Francisco: Harper & Row, 1984.
The Guardian of the Threshold. Transl. by Ruth Pusch and Hans Pusch. Toronto: Steiner Book Centre, 1973.
Ein Malerischer Schulungsweg. Dornach, Switzerland: Rudolf Steiner Press, 1986.
Occult Signs and Symbols. New York: Anthroposophic Press, 1972.
The Souls' Awakening. Transl. by Ruth Pusch and Hans Pusch. Toronto: Steiner Book Centre, 1973.

Stern, Jane, and Michael Stern, *Amazing America*. New York: Random House, 1978.

Taylor, Anne, *Visions of Harmony*. New York: Oxford University Press, 1987.

Taylor, Thomas, transl., *Iamblichus' Life of Pythagoras*. Rochester, Vt.: Inner Traditions International, 1986 (reprint of 1818 edition).

Teilhard de Chardin, Pierre, *The Heart of Matter*. Transl. by René Hague. New York: Harcourt Brace Jovanovich, 1978.

Thomas, Robert David, *The Man Who Would Be Perfect*. Philadelphia: University of Pennsylvania Press, 1977.

Thorndike, Joseph J., Jr., "Fruitlands." *American Heritage*, February-March 1986.

Tisdall, Caroline, and Angelo Bozzolla, *Futurism*. New York: Oxford University Press, 1978.

Tompkins, C. "Profiles: Michael Murphy." *The New Yorker*, January 5, 1976.

Tompkins, Peter, and Christopher Bird, *Secrets of the Soil*. San Francisco: Harper & Row, 1989.

Turner, J. F., "Howard Finster's Paradise Garden." *Raw Vision* (London), winter 1989-1990.

"Twenty-One Years of Auroville: A Village View." *Auroville Today* (Tamil Nandu, India), February 28, 1989.

Vahle, Neal, "Esalen Celebrates Its Silver Anniversary." *New Realities*. September-October 1987.

Viera, Ricardo, and Norman Girardot, *The Worlds Folk Art Church: Reverend Howard Finster and Family* (exhibition catalog). Bethlehem, Pa.: Lehigh University Art Galleries, 1986.

Visionary Architects: Boullée, Ledoux, Lequeu. Houston, Tex.: University of St. Thomas, 1968.

Vogel, C. J. de, *Pythagoras and Early Pythagoreanism*. Netherlands: Van Gorcum, 1966.

Wachsmuth, Guenther, *The Life and Work of Rudolf Steiner from the Turn of the Century to His Death*. Transl. by Olin D. Wannamaker and Reginald E. Raab. New York: Whittier Books, 1955.

Walker, Kenneth, *Venture with Ideas*. London: Jonathan Cape, 1951.

Ward, Fred, "In Long-Forbidden Tibet." *National Geographic*, February 1980.

Webb, James, *The Harmonious Circle*. New York: G. P. Putnam's Sons, 1980.

Welch, Stuart Cary, *India: Art and Culture, 1300-1900*. New York: Holt, Rinehart and Winston, 1985.

Westwood, Jennifer, ed., *The Atlas of Mysterious Places*. New York: Weidenfeld & Nicolson, 1987.

White, Anna, and Leila S. Taylor, *Shakerism*. New York: AMS Press, 1971.

Whitford, Frank, *Bauhaus*. London: Thames and Hudson, 1984.

Wilfried, *The Mother: A Short Biography*. Pondicherry, India: Sri Aurobindo Society, 1986.

William Morris Today (exhibition catalog). London: Institute of Contemporary Arts, 1984.

Wilson, Colin, *G. I. Gurdjieff.* Wellingborough, Northamptonshire, England: Aquarian Press, 1986.

Wosien, Maria-Gabriele, *Sacred Dance: Encounter with the Gods.* New York: Avon, 1974.

Wright, Frank Lloyd, *An Autobiography.* New York: Horizon Press, 1932.

Wright, Lawrence, "Part Three: Inner Peace." *Rolling Stone,* November 16, 1989.

Wright, Olgivanna Lloyd, *The Shining Brow: Frank Lloyd Wright.* New York: Horizon Press, 1960.

Wythe, Iain Boyd:
Bruno Taut and the Architecture of Activism. Cambridge: Cambridge University Press, 1982.
Glass Chain Letters: Architectural Fantasies by Bruno Taut and His Circle. Cambridge, Mass.: MIT Press, 1985.

PICTURE CREDITS

The sources for the illustrations in this book are listed below. Credits from left to right are separated by semicolons, from top to bottom by dashes.

Cover art by Greg Harlin of Stansbury, Ronsaville, Wood, Inc. 6: The Chester Beatty Library, Dublin. 7: Courtesy the Arthur M. Sackler Gallery, Smithsonian Institution, Washington, D.C. 8: Jean-Louis Nou, Paris. 9: Bildarchiv Preussischer Kulturbesitz, West Berlin. 10, 11: The Metropolitan Museum of Art, the Sackler Fund (1969 69.242.10.); Bofutenmangu, Bofu, Yamaguchi Prefecture, courtesy Tokyo National Musuem, Japan. 12, 13: Scala, Florence, courtesy Galleria degli Uffizi, Florence; the Bridgeman Art Library, London. 14, 15: The Tate Gallery, London. 17: Art by Kim Barnes of Stansbury, Ronsaville, Wood, Inc. 18, 19: Courtesy the National Portrait Gallery, London; Archiv für Kunst und Geschichte, West Berlin; courtesy the British Library, London. 20, 21: The Bridgeman Art Library, London. 22: Scala, Florence, courtesy Memling Museum, Bruges. 24: Kay Chernush/Image Bank—Sonia Halliday Photographs, Weston Turville, Buckinghamshire. 26, 27: Galen Rowell/Mountain Light. 29: Scala, Florence, courtesy Fosco Maraini Collection, Florence. 30: Mary Evans Picture Library, London. 32: Bibliothèque Nationale, Paris. 34: Bildarchiv Preussischer Kulturbesitz, West Berlin. 35: National Portrait Gallery, London. 36, 37: The William Morris Gallery, London; Victoria and Albert Museum, London; the E. T. Archive/Tate Gallery, London, background the William Morris Gallery, London. 38: The Hulton-Deutsch Collection, London; the City of Manchester Art Galleries, London, background the William Morris Gallery, London. 40, 41: Worcester Art Museum, Worcester, Mass. 43: Photo by Jonathan Williams, from *St. Eom in the Land of Pasaquan* by Tom Patterson, the Jargon Society, Columbus, Ga., 1987. 44, 45: Productions Clovis Prévost—from *Le Palais Idéal du Facteur Cheval* by Jean Pierre Jouve, Claude Prévost, Clovis Prévost © Éditions du Moniteur, Paris, 1981, background photo Archives de la Drôme. 46, 47: From *St. Eom in the Land of Pasaquan* by Tom Patterson, the Jargon Society, Columbus, Ga., 1987—from *St. Eom in the Land of Pasaquan* by Tom Patterson, the Jargon Society, Columbus, Ga., 1987, courtesy Roger Manley; Jonathan Williams. 48, 49: Copyright Roger Manley. 50, 51: From *Fantastic Architecture: Personal and Eccentric Visions* by Michael Schuyt, Harry N. Abrams, New York, 1980, except upper left Robert Doisneau/Ralpho, Paris. 52, 53: Gregg Blasdel (2), background photo Joe Covello/Black Star. 54, 55: Explorer, Par-

is, except upper left Dmitri Kessel, Paris. 57: Art by Kim Barnes of Stansbury, Ronsaville, Wood, Inc. 58, 59: Courtesy Church Archives, the Church of Jesus Christ of Latter-day Saints, except center the Church of Jesus Christ of Latter-day Saints, Visual Resources Library, Salt Lake City, Utah. 61: Photo by Cliff Roenh, courtesy Pennsylvania Historical and Museum Commission, Old Economy Village, Ambridge, Pa.—Indiana Historical Society, William Henry Smith Memorial Library (#4485). 62: New York State Museum, Albany, New York. 63: Collection of the United Society of Shakers, Sabbathday Lake, Maine. 64, 65: Fruitlands Museums, Massachusetts. 66, 67: Courtesy William Helfand; collection of the United Society of Shakers, Sabbathday Lake, Maine; Henry Groskinsky, courtesy Milton Sherman (8). 68: Western Reserve Historical Society, Cleveland. 69: New York State Museum, Albany, New York; the Shaker Museum, Old Chatham, New York. 70: The Shaker Museum, Old Chatham, New York. 71: Hancock Shaker Village. 72: Hancock Shaker Village (2)—Collection of the United Society of Shakers, Sabbathday Lake, Maine; Western Reserve Historical Society, Cleveland. 76: Oneida Community Mansion House, New York. 78, 79: Columbia University Libraries, Harris Oliphant Collection. 80, 81: From *Facing the Light* by Harold Francis Pfister, published for the National Portrait Gallery by Smithsonian Institution Press, Washington, D.C., 1978 (3); Library of Congress. 82: Painting by Josiah Woolcott, courtesy Massachusetts Historical Society. 83: Copied by Mark Sexton, courtesy the Orchard House, Concord, Mass. 84: From *Art and Glory: The Story of Elbert Hubbard* by Freeman Champney, Crown, New York, 1968. 85: Copied by Larry Sherer, courtesy Roycroft Associates; Roycroft Associates. 86-97: Archives, the Theosophical Society, Pasadena, Calif. 99: Art by Kim Barnes of Stansbury, Ronsaville, Wood, Inc. 100: Bettmann Archive/UPI Newsphotos; from *The Harmonious Circle: The Lives and Work of G. I. Gurdjieff, P. D. Ouspensky, and Their Followers* by James Webb, G. P. Putnam's Sons, New York, 1980. 102, 103: © Farrell Grehan/Photo Researchers. 104: From *An American Architecture* by Frank Lloyd Wright, edited by Edgar Kaufmann, © Horizon Press, New York, 1955—the Frank Lloyd Wright Archives, © the Frank Lloyd Wright Foundation. 105: From *Gurdjieff: Making a New World* by John G. Bennett; © 1973, published by Turnstone Books, London, 1973. 106: From *Teachings of Gurdjieff* by C. S. Nott, Routledge & Kegan Paul, London, 1961. 107: Artwork by Time-Life Books, Inc. 108: From *The Harmonious Circle: The Lives and Work of G. I. Gurdjieff, P. D. Ouspensky, and Their Followers* by James Webb, G. P. Putnam's Sons,

New York, 1980—from *Journey through This World: The Second Journal of a Pupil* by S. C. Nott, Routledge & Kegan Paul, London, 1969. 109: From *Gurdjieff and Mansfield* by James Moore, Routledge & Kegan Paul, London, 1980. 110: Süddeutscher Verlag Bilderdienst, Munich. 111: From *Art Inspired by Rudolf Steiner* by John Fletcher, © Mercury Arts, 1987. 112-115: Rudolf Steiner Verlag, Dornach, Switzerland. 116, 117: Museo Comarcal de Reus, copied by Catalá-Roca, Barcelona; Catalá-Roca—René Roland, Le Vésinet, France. 118, 119: Rudolf Steiner Verlag, Dornach, Switzerland. 120, 121: Erich Lessing, Vienna, courtesy the Hablik Collection; © 1990 Familien Nachlass Oskar Schlemmer, Badenweiler. 122: Giraudon, Paris. 123: Copied by Luca Carrà, Milan, courtesy Collection of Angelo Calmarini, Milan—copied by Vivi Papi, Varese, courtesy Fondazione Russolo-Pratella, Varese. 124, 125: Tretyakov Gallery; Ilse Berg—Kazimir Malevich Suprematist Composition: White on White 1918 Collection, the Museum of Modern Art, New York; Indiana University Art Museum, Bloomington, Ind. (#77.55.2). 126, 127: Akademie der Kunste Berlin, Sammlung Baukunst, except lower right Wenzel-Hablik-Stiftung, Itzehoe. 128, 129: Bauhaus-Archiv, Berlin, © VG Bild-Kunst; courtesy Agfa Foto Historama, Cologne—Bauhaus-Archiv, West Berlin. 130: Besitzangabe, Collection: Kunsthaus Zurich; Bauhaus-Archiv; from *Klee,* by Denys Chevalier, Crown, New York, 1979, courtesy ARS, New York/COSMOPRESS—Hugo Erfurth, Agfa Foto-Historama, Cologne. 131: Bildarchiv Preussischer Kulturbesitz, West Berlin; © 1990 Theater Nachlass Oskar Schlemmer, Sammlung UJS Badenweiler; Fotografische Sammlung Museum Museum Folkwang, Essen—Musée National D'Art Moderne, Centre National d'Art et de Culture Georges Pompidou, Paris. 132, 133: Municipal Museum the Hague; Stedelijk Museum, Amsterdam (2)—Produktie Grafische Afdeling, Capi-Lux Vak; Bauhaus-Archiv, West Berlin. 135: Artwork by Kim Barnes of Stansbury, Ronsaville, Wood, Inc. 136: © Joyce Lyke/Esalen Media Center—Michael Alexander for LIFE. 138, 139: Paul Fusco/Magnum Photos. 140, 141: Sergio Stingo, Milan; Comunità Damanhur, Turin; Sergio Stingo, Milan. 142, 143: From *Linking the Future: Findhorn, Auroville, Arcosanti* by Jerome Clayton Glenn, Hexiad Project, Cambridge, Mass., 1979. 145: From *Faces of Findhorn: Images of a Planetary Family* by the Findhorn Community, Harper & Row, San Francisco, 1980. 146, 147: Dominique Darr, Paris. 148, 149: Dominique Darr, Paris (2); Guy Piacentino. 150, 151: The Buckminster Fuller Institute, Los Angeles, background artwork by Time-Life Books, Inc.

INDEX

Time-Life Books Inc.
is a wholly owned subsidiary of
THE TIME INC. BOOK COMPANY

President and Chief Executive Officer: Kelso F. Sutton
President, Time Inc. Books Direct: Christopher T. Linen

TIME-LIFE BOOKS INC.

EDITOR: George Constable
Director of Design: Louis Klein
Director of Editorial Resources: Phyllis K. Wise
Director of Photography and Research: John Conrad Weiser

PRESIDENT: John M. Fahey, Jr.
Senior Vice Presidents: Robert M. DeSena, Paul R. Stewart,
Curtis G. Viebranz, Joseph J. Ward
Vice Presidents: Stephen L. Bair, Bonita L. Boezeman,
Mary P. Donohoe, Stephen L. Goldstein, Juanita T. James,
Andrew P. Kaplan, Trevor Lunn, Susan J. Maruyama,
Robert H. Smith
New Product Development: Trevor Lunn, Donia Ann Steele
Supervisor of Quality Control: James King

PUBLISHER: Joseph J. Ward

Editorial Operations
Production: Celia Beattie
Library: Louise D. Forstall
Computer Composition: Gordon E. Buck (Manager),
Deborah G. Tait, Monika D. Thayer, Janet Barnes Syring,
Lillian Daniels

Library of Congress Cataloging in Publication Data

Utopian Visions by the editors of Time-Life Books.
p. cm.—(Mysteries of the unknown.)
Includes bibliographical references.
ISBN 0-8094-6376-8   ISBN 0-8094-6377-6 (lib. bdg.)
1. Utopias—History.   I. Time-Life Books.   II. Series.
HX806.U79344 1990   90-35512
355'.02—dc20   CIP

MYSTERIES OF THE UNKNOWN

SERIES DIRECTOR: Jim Hicks
Series Administrator: Myrna Traylor-Herndon
Designer: Tom Huestis

Editorial Staff for *Utopian Visions*
Associate Editors: Sarah Schneidman (pictures);
Janet Cave (text)
Text Editor: Robert A. Doyle
Researchers: Patti H. Cass, Constance Contreras,
Sharon Obermiller, Carla Reissman
Staff Writers: Margery A. duMond, Marfé Ferguson Delano
Assistant Designer: Susan M. Gibas
Copy Coordinators: Mary Beth Oelkers-Keegan,
Colette Stockum (principal); John Weber
Picture Coordinator: Leanne G. Miller
Editorial Assistant: Donna Fountain

Special Contributors: Susan M. Schaeffer (lead research);
Beth DeFrancis, Patricia A. Paterno, Evelyn S. Prettyman,
Priscilla T. Schneidman, Joann Stern (research); Champ
Clark, John Clausen, George Daniels, Norman Draper,
Alison Kahn, Robert Kiener, Harvey S. Loomis, Brian J.
McGinn, Wendy Murphy, Jake Page, Curtis W. Pendergast,
Susan Perry, Peter Pocock, James Schutze, Daniel
Stashower, Danna L. Walker, May Wuthrich (text); John
Drummond (design); Hazel Blumberg-McKee (index)

Correspondents: Elisabeth Kraemer-Singh (Bonn), Christine
Hinze (London), Christina Lieberman (New York), Maria
Vincenza Aloisi (Paris), Ann Natanson (Rome).
Valuable assistance was also provided by Angelika
Lemmer (Bonn); Judy Aspinall, Lesley Coleman (London);
Trini Bandrés (Madrid); Elizabeth Brown (New York); Ann
Wise (Rome); Mary Johnson (Stockholm); Traudl Lessing
(Vienna).

Consultant:
Marcello Truzzi, general consultant for the series, is a
professor of sociology at Eastern Michigan University. He
is also director of the Center for Scientific Anomalies
Research (CSAR) and editor of its journal, the *Zetetic
Scholar*. Dr. Truzzi, who considers himself a "constructive
skeptic" with regard to claims of the paranormal, works
through the CSAR to produce dialogues between critics
and proponents of unusual scientific claims.

Other Publications:

AMERICAN COUNTRY
THE THIRD REICH
VOYAGE THROUGH THE UNIVERSE
THE TIME-LIFE GARDENER'S GUIDE
TIME FRAME
FIX IT YOURSELF
FITNESS, HEALTH & NUTRITION
SUCCESSFUL PARENTING
HEALTHY HOME COOKING
UNDERSTANDING COMPUTERS
LIBRARY OF NATIONS
THE ENCHANTED WORLD
THE KODAK LIBRARY OF CREATIVE PHOTOGRAPHY
GREAT MEALS IN MINUTES
THE CIVIL WAR
PLANET EARTH
COLLECTOR'S LIBRARY OF THE CIVIL WAR
THE EPIC OF FLIGHT
THE GOOD COOK
WORLD WAR II
HOME REPAIR AND IMPROVEMENT
THE OLD WEST

*For information on and a full description of any of the Time-
Life Books series listed above, please call 1-800-621-7026 or
write:*
Reader Information
Time-Life Customer Service
P.O. Box C-32068
Richmond, Virginia 23261-2068

This volume is one of a series that examines the history
and nature of seemingly paranormal phenomena. Other
books in the series include:

Time-Life Books Inc. offers a wide range of fine record-
ings, including a *Rock 'n' Roll Era* series. For subscription
information, call 1-800-621-7026 or write Time-Life Music, P.O. Box C-32068, Richmond, Virginia 23261-2068.